In his official role as Senior Party Consultant for Bud Light beer, jet-setting executive Spuds MacKenzie doesn't have to take any "bull" from anyone. But despite his sophisticated ways and enigmatic countenance, Spuds is really a softie at heart, not a "terrier" at all. Whether hanging ten off Maui or dancing the night away with a succession of beautiful women, Spuds handles every situation with the greatest aplomb. Listen up, all you Spuds fans, and learn how he does it. A look at the individual behind the legend and a closeup of his fabulous wardrobe are featured in six exclusive CQ pages (pp. 18-23).

CQ

FASHION

FEATURES

DEPARTMENTS

OHIO
STATE

40/An old yarn with a new twist

68/Dash away, all

6/Masculine mystique

 For information address The Main Street Press, William Case House, Pittstown, New Jersey 08867.

Library of Congress Cataloging-in-Publication Data

Schell, Ina.
CQ : a parody of the world's most elegant magazine for men.

1. Dogs--Humor. I. GQ II. Title.
PN6231.D68S34 1987
818'.5407 87-21696
ISBN 1-55562-035-3 (Pbk.)

FIRST EDITION 1987

Jacket and text design by Frank Mahood.

87 88 89 90 91 10 9 8 7 6 5 4 3 2 1

PUBLISHED BY THE MAIN STREET PRESS, PITTSTOWN, NEW JERSEY

CQ

Author **INA SCHELL**

Designer **FRANK MAHOOD**

Production Editor JOHN D. FOX
Fashion TONY BANKERT, HUNTINGTON BARCLAY, LYNN CHASE, MARSHA FELTINGOFF, CYNTHIA GILLETTE FOX, GERRY FRIEDMANN, BILL JULIAN, JANE KAHN, HONEY LORING, PAM LUBY, MIKE McDEVITT, ALICE NICHOLS, LYNN NOVEMBER, BARBARA PAHIOS, DEE PRINCE, JOE RICHTER, ANN SALE, TOM SCHUMACHER, JACKIE SPERANDIO, JACK TAYLOR, KAREN THOMPSON, LONA THOMPSON, TOKKY, LEIGH WESTBROOK, CHUCK WILLIMAN, LESLIE YELLIN
Grooming JAMES BERRY, JOHN MALENGA, JOHN NASH, VAL PENSTONE, HARVEY REICH, JOHN STAZKO, JERRY SHENBERG
Fitness DAVIA ANNE GALLUP, STUART ROGERS, JOAN SCHULTZ, CAROL TELLMAN

Publisher **LAWRENCE GROW**

Sales Manager DONALD ROLFE
Direct Response MARIANN ARNITZ, TOM LAND
Wheels PETER W. GLASSER
Public Relations PEGGY RAUB
Chief Photographer BRADLEY OLMAN
Photographers ROGER APPLEBY, DAN BARBA, WALTER CHANDOHA, CARLA HOTVEDT, JAMES PIPKIN, RAEANNE RUBENSTEIN, CHARLES C. VARGA
Travel ROBERT LEEDS, MAURICE MOORMAN, BONNIE SCHACTER, WALTER M. WOOLF
Models APOLLO, ATHENA, BARNIE, BO, BOO BOO, BOOMER, CASEY, CASSIE, CINNAMON, DOMINO, FAUST, GOLIATH, HANNA, HELD, JACKPOT, KEEGAN, KITTY, KNIGHT, LADY, McDUFF, NIKI, RADAR, REMINGTON, SACKETT, SALLY, SCHULTZ, SCHATZEE, SKY-STRIDER, SPICE, TEX, WARWICK'S JEREMY
Interiors LOREN BEAVER, DOROTHY CASHMERE, DAVE FAIR, CANNON GARBER, PAM HUDAK
Cuisine LINDA COFFEY, RICK SMILOW, BERNARD TONKEN, ALEX VILLETAS

Managing Editor **VICKI BROOKS**
Senior Editor **KIRSTIN OLSEN**

CQ's Favorites PAMELA & HOWARD ABRAHAMS, BONNIE AIKMAN, KATE ALFRIEND, BONNIE BERGIN, DAVID N. BERKWITZ, ANDRA BOLIKER, ALBERT BRUNO, CRYSTAL CARNESE, JOY CHRISTOV, DAN CHURCH, JULIA CONAGHAN, BRUCE COOK, CHRIS CROSS, JOHN DANKO, JOHN DAVENPORT, ROBIN DIXON, ELAINE FARRANT, SUZANNE FARRELL, DENNIS FETKO, LAURA FISHER, JEFF GREEN, MICHELLE GREENBERG, SANDY HARRINGTON, JOANNE HARTZOG, GLENDA HERRO, JEFFREY HON, JOHN JAVNA, JEFF KAPLAN, TOM McLAUGHLIN, DOUG McLENNAN, AMORY MILLARD, JULIA MOSCOVE, JIM ORSO, VICKI PERLMAN, CARMELITA POPE, HOWARD REHS, SHELLEY & LARRY REMALY, CHET SCHULTZ III, MELISSA SCHULTZ, PAT SCHULTZ, RUTH SHAFFER, DENISE SIBOLE, BARBARA SKINNER, BRAD STACKHOUSE, BILL STOLBERG, BRUCE TOBIN, VAL TYLER, SUSAN VEIDT, RON YOGMAN

Editorial Director **MARTIN GREIF**

PRINTED IN JAPAN FIRST PRINTING, AUGUST, 1987
Published by The Main Street Press, William Case House, Pittstown, New Jersey 08867
Published simultaneously in Canada by Methuen Publications, 2330 Midland Avenue, Agincourt, Ontario M1S 1P7

Library of Congress Cataloging-in-Publication Data
Schell, Ina.
CQ : a parody of the world's most elegant magazine for men.
1. Dogs--Humor. I. GQ II. Title.
PN6231.D68S34 1987 818'.5407 87-21696
ISBN 1-55562-035-3 (Pbk.)

LETTERS

A Dog's Best Friend?

Thank you for your recent article dispelling the myth that dogs and cats are natural enemies. We *can* get along with each other if we're willing to give it a chance. I gave up chasing cats four years ago, and they've been the best four years of my life. I finally have time to chase more deserving things, like tennis balls and squirrels, and I've developed valuable friendships with several cats. It's high time all of us shook paws and let the flying fur settle. Congratulations on a bold, laudable stand.

TOM HARRIER
STAMFORD, CONN.

What's happening to this country? I worry about the state of my society when a reputable publication like *CQ* thinks it can get away with an equal-rights-for-cats sermon. Your lopsided article presented only the cats' side of the story. What about the scratched noses of my friends? What about the openly belligerent hissing and unsheathed claws I encounter every day? Cats don't want a cease-fire; they're just waiting for uncanine dogma like yours to muzzle us so that they can attack us at our most vulnerable. I'd sooner take a trip to the vet's than trust a sneaky feline.

G. SHEPHERD
CHICAGO, IL.

Your piece on easing tension between dogs and cats was undoubtedly inspired by good motives, but the naiveté of the author is lamentable. Bark all you like, but I, for one, am not coming down from my twenty-foot white pine until I see some positive action on the part of dogs—or a sturdy fence or leash keeping them in their proper place.

KITTY WILLIAMS
CATTANOOGA, TENN.

The Long and Short of It

I loved your article on Michael J. Foxhound even though it never explains why, despite his short stature, females seem to swoon over him. I'm a Corgi passionately in love with a Mastiff bitch, yet she won't even sniff at me. What's Foxhound got that I haven't?

BANTAM CORGI
LONDON, ENGLAND

Michael J. Foxhound says that when you're rolling in dog biscuits nobody cares whether you're a Chihuahua or a Great Dane.

Howling Success

Your profile of Bruce Springersteen was wonderful. I've been a fan of his purebred talent and street-mongrel grittiness for years. His "Whelped in the U.S.A." occupies a special place in my record collection—and in my heart. Thanks for your interview, and for your photographs, which show just how sexy a dog can look in denim.

FLUFFY GIANELLI
SOUTH AMBOY, N.J.

Co-Ed Canines

Now that Brooke Shields has graduated from Princeton, and Jody Foster from Yale, can you tell me how this hot and humpy Labrador Retriever can get into Barnard College?

KNIGHT VARGA
FRENCHTOWN, N.J.

Take the number 7 Broadway line to the 116th Street station, walk upstairs, find 606 West 120th Street, and knock on the door.

Dogs in the Manger

The appalling religious dogfight depicted in your article on Jim and Tammy Barker had me whining in despair, not only because of the puppyish behavior of the humans involved, but also for the dogs whose deluded owners deprived them of the comforts of life in order to send money to the Barkers.

B. SHAWN FRISÉ
MIAMI, FLA.

I was certainly shocked by your coverage of the Barker scandal, but the photos of the Barker mansion did give me a good idea. How can I get my people to spring for an air-conditioned doghouse? It would be perfect for summer entertaining!

D. PINSCHER
MUTTEREY, CALIF.

You could try a little charm and a lot ot tongue-lolling, but if it's a choice between having air-conditioning or owners like the Barkers, we'd advise you to take the heat.

CQ's CDs

As an avid *CQ* reader, I've noticed that your Letters column always sandwiches a question about stereo sets between comments about movie stars, shoulder pads, or double-breasted blue blazers. Are there really dummies out there who write to you instead of visiting their local stereo shops, or do you guys write these letters yourselves to suggest that *CQ*'s readers are interested in more than sex and clothes?

IVAN BARKSKY
NEW YORK CITY

People who live in glass doghouses shouldn't throw stones.

Raised Hackles Over Colorization

Whoever wrote your piece in Off the Collar about the colorization of Rin-Tin-Tin films is barking up the wrong tree. Colorization is harmless, and it's nice to see my favorite old-movie star as he was in real life. Besides, colorization attracts whole generations of young dogs who have never seen the master at work. If the great Shepherd were alive today, he'd rather be appreciated in color than ignored in black-and-white.

PUG LEWIS
BITTEN ROUGE, LA.

My thanks for your article on colorization. When film legends like Woofy Allen and Ginger Rovers sit up and bark, I listen. They're absolutely right; faced with an aesthetic tragedy like the mutilation of classic movies, we cannot roll over and play dead.

SCOTTIE MACKAY
GRRREEN BAY, WISC.

Has anyone on your editorial staff considered the fact that dogs can't even see in color?

C.F.N. AFGHAN
LOS ANGELES, CALIF.

Pee-Wee's Doghouse

I loved your feature on TV's Pee-Wee Hounddog, but I'm still puzzled about one thing. What exactly is Pee-Wee's relationship with Miss Yvonne?

GARY HEARTWORM
WASHINGTON, D.C.

Neither is talking, but the Miami Herald *has reported that they both use the same face powder.*

Candy-Coated Review

Your review of Mel Brooks's new movie, *Spaceballs*, completely ignored the film's most revolting character—a half-man, half-dog monstrosity called a "mog." Having read your article, and utterly ignorant of what I would be forced to see, I went to see the movie, and I was disgusted. The idea of such a creature existing is sickening enough—imagine the greed and selfishness of humanity being visible on canine features!—but John Candy, the actor who played the mog, took the outrage a step farther by *objecting* to being mistaken for a dog! How can a self-respecting dog patronize a film that so discredits his own species? I'm proud to say that I walked out of the movie, and I did so on all fours, unlike the so-called mog, which paraded around on its hind legs.

O.E. SHEEPDOG
MIDDLEBURY, VT.

Why didn't your review of *Spaceballs* say something about John Candy? I've always been a fan of his, but he's never looked better than he does in this movie. The ears, paws, and tail drove me crazy.

KAY NIGHN
TAMPA, FLA.

Wamsetter BATH SHEETS

CANDY STRIPES IN LUSCIOUS COLORS: Liver Rouge and Beefbone Tan • Kibble Brown and Rawhide Beige • Ken-L Red and Flea-Collar White

© WALTER CHANDOHA

THE BATH SHOP bloomingdog's

CQ&A

Hold the phone—Benji realizes he can save the trouble of dialing and send a card instead.

I have a terrible time with fleas. . . they seem to be particularly tenacious here in the still-wild West. Shampoos, sprays, and dips get most of them, but somehow a few always remain to torment me. Any suggestions? LHASA L'AMOUR, FURGO, N.D.

Sure. Peak's Mister Flea comb is perfect for your fine, thick hair. It has 32 flat teeth to the inch, rather than the typical comb's 28 round ones, to give maximum penetration of the fur, and will remove both the nasty little buggers and the eggs they've laid. Mister Flea is available at your local pet shop, or contact Peak Pet Products, 400 Quaint Acres Dr., Silver Spring, MD 20904, for the name of an outlet near you.

How can I find appropriate greeting cards to send to my canine friends? Yes, I know there are lots of cards to send to special humans, but what about us dogs? Doesn't anybody care? We like to remember each other's birthdays and anniversaries too, you know.

SHEBA BROOKS, ST. PETERSBURG, FLA.

We know. And so does Innovative Amenities. The company has filled that void for you with a good selection of cards for dogs from dogs. Subjects include the usual ones (getting well, birthday, anniversary), but also some special events that only dogs can appreciate: completion of paper training or obedience school, for instance. Innovative Amenities cards are available at gift, pet, and stationery shops, or contact: Innovative Amenities, Inc., 1021 Lincoln Blvd., Suite 217, Santa Monica, CA 90403, (213) 394-6992.

My vet tells me that I'm highly allergic to the chemicals in most generally available flea dips. But where I live, dahlings, the nasty little creatures are a problem year-round, and mild shampoos don't scare them one bit. Help! I'm in torture!

CHOW CHOW GABOR, DANESVILLE, FLA.

Suffer no more. The savvy chemists at Natural Products Supply have just what you need: a lemony-mint flea-repellent oil distilled from natural pennyroyal, citronella, and eucalyptus. Just five or ten drops on your brush once a week will keep that coat flea-free and fragrant. And there's a sachet to tuck in a corner of your bed. The company guarantees its flea repellent to be completely effective and absolutely non-toxic, or your money back. Contact Natural Products Supply Company, 24 E. Burd St., Shippensburg, PA 17257, (717) 532-2566.

I'm an avid reader and of course passionately interested in any books about dogs, but I've just heard that a new animal parody of *Cosmopolitan* magazine has been published and that it's absolutely hilarious. Can you tell me somthing about it?

BUTCH TOBIN, SOLEBURY, PENNA.

You must have in mind *Cowsmopolitan*, a bovine take-off of *Cosmo* and an udder riot. The parody, a dead-ringer for the original, is supposedly edited by "Helen Guernsey Brown" and features such *Cosmo*-like articles as "Lose 600 Pounds in Just 3 Weeks." For information about this very clever satire, contact *Cowsmopolitan's* publisher, Day Dream Publishing, 315 West Haley Street, Santa Barbara, CA 93101, (805) 966-1551.

I read in the papers that ALPO Petfoods has sponsored a contest to select the best "doggerel about dogs," but I never read anything about the winner. Can you enlighten me?

OGDEN GNASH, GNASHVILLE, TENN.

Richard Headley, of Thousand Oaks, California, won one-half ton of ALPO dog food as top dog in the "ALPO Dog Days of August Doggerel Write-Off." His winning entry was "Woof-out at Bow-wow Corral," which reads in part:

> The anxious crowd was yapping loud
> at the bar in Red-dog Inn.
> The time will arrive promptly at five
> when the contest is due to begin.
>
> Standing alone sniffing a bone
> is the challenger Hangdog Fred.
> On the other side showing snooty pride
> is the champion Top-dog Ted.

The rest of the poem, portraying a canine "woof-out" a la Gary Cooper in *High Noon*, perfectly exemplifies doggerel as loose verse written for comic effect. Richard Headley very kindly donated his half-ton of ALPO to a guide dog school for the blind—International Guiding Eyes, 13445 Glen Oaks Boulevard, Sylmar, Calif.

My people are trying to convince me to take a cross-country trip with them, but I'm hesitant. I'm not sure that traveling will be to my taste or that the available accommodations will meet my standards. What can I expect?

SALLY GROW, PITTSTOWN, NJ.

You're in luck. Read Greyhound Greene's article on travel in this issue of *CQ*.

I don't mean to sound unpatriotic, but I've always preferred the cut of European clothes to the rather ready-made look of even expensive American fashions. I've bought clothing in London and in Paris, and now I'll soon be taking the air in Switzerland. Can you recommend a shop that will make me look as if I have my own Swiss bank account?

CRANFORD STEWARD, BERKELEY, CALIF.

Continental dogs are barking about Prima, the most exclusive canine salon in Switzerland. Visit Prima at 9 rue Pichard, CH-1003 Lausanne, Telephone:021-22-10-06. Prima's sweaters and coats will make you look like a Wall Street arbitrager.

Why I wear what I wear

ACTING IS EASY, DRESSING EVEN EASIER

To some, Lucky Dog's Ike is a media sensation. To some, he is a forbidding bundle of muscle, jowls, and wrinkles. But it only takes a look into those dark brown eyes to know that there's more to Ike than his image. In fact, it was his eyes that got him his current job. "From the moment we saw Ike's soulful eyes," said Lucky Dog's product manager A. Peter Barbaresi, "we knew he was the right choice." Barbaresi could also have mentioned Ike's throaty, jovial voice, his intelligence, and his good nature. Ike is one of those rare figures in the entertainment business—a talented, successful actor who hasn't lost his charming modesty or his sense of perspective. He downplays his success, giving the credit, with a paw-in-the-sand puppyishness, to luck and the loyal devotion of some fine humans. Asked if he considers himself a star, Ike shrinks from the term in surprise: "Me? Not a chance. The dogs who played Rin-Tin-Tin, Lassie, and Old Yeller—*they* were stars. They were the greats. They made magic, and you just don't see acting like that anymore. We've all gotten too lazy to go for that extra stunt, to pull that extra tear from the audience. I'm just a character actor who got lucky, that's all."

But Ike is a star, and he's having to get used to it. In a way, he seems to have been destined to succeed in the glittery world of show business. His mother, Kay, appeared with Clint Eastwoof in "Sudden Impact," and Ike was born during the filming. Ike's own long list of credits includes both film and television roles.

When you called attention to your sweatshirt in your debut Lucky Dog commercial, you became the first canine celebrity to make a pointed fashion statement. Why did you choose this particular statement?

IKE: I like comfortable clothes. I've always liked them. And I didn't see any reason to change my style for the commercials. Besides, a spokesdog shouldn't be intimidating. Other dogs have to like me, and it's harder to like a guy in a three-piece suit than in a sweatshirt.

How do you liven up your wardrobe?

I have a very strong sense of the absurd. I'll put on almost anything when I'm feeling like a change, from dark sunglasses to a gaudy bow tie to a hat with a propeller. I don't mind looking a little silly now and then.

Ike's informal elegance can help to put the "You" back in "Casual."

Do you have a fitness program?

Do I look like I have a fitness program? I sit on the couch a lot. Sometimes I read or watch soap operas. About the most athletic thing I do is football. Watching it, not playing it.

What do you wear to dress up?

A dark sweatshirt.

How would you sum up your sartorial philosophy?

If it feels good, wear it.

Elements of Style

PUTTING ON THE DOG

Only a breath away from the Windy City, the town of Long Grove takes pride in its history. But, nestled in this suburban environment, hidden behind a quaint and unassuming facade, lies a shop that represents the cutting edge of canine fashion. It's the Dog House, and it's responsible for the sartorial awakening of the midwestern dog.

The colors demand your attention from the moment you enter. The Dog House is awash in waves of intense color crashing against a shoreline of neutral tones. A soft gray coat lined with fire-hydrant red corduroy and trimmed with black buttons awaits a dog who knows how to wear it; a classic khaki trenchcoat sports a predominantly red plaid lining. Eventually, red and black emerge as the favored colors. Dramatic red coats with black trim or details and striking fashions in solid black draw the eye.

The Dog House was founded in the mid-sixties by Charles W. Mercer—partly because he knew dogs who had trouble finding the combination of quality and style they demanded and partly to keep himself busy after his retirement. "I started with one major supplier," he once said, "then added new merchandise as I heard of other things made for dogs." In the search for new designs to feature, the Dog House took some chances and became known for the breathtaking variety of its clothing and accessories. The store has carried lumberjack coats, sailors' and firemen's uniforms, snowsuits, 18K gold-plated collars, jewel-studded collars and leads, tuxedos, sweaters imported from Switzerland, raincoats, boots, pajamas, a camel's hair coat with a raccoon collar, and hats of almost every description. For the dog who wants to live the total Dog House lifestyle, there are toys, beds, car seats, I.D. tags, nail files, brushes, clippers, shampoos, vitamins, deodorants, breath fresheners, and snacks. Mercer concentrated on finding the perfect style for each customer. The fit of a garment, he said, wasn't everything: "Even if it fits, it might not look right. What looks good on one dog might not look good on another."

The store, now owned by Mrs. Mildred Mercer and managed by Barbara Pahios, continues its tradition of attentive service and trendsetting fashion. It remains a favorite with high-profile hounds and purebreds with panache. Even the mutt who's arrived arrives there first. The Dog House is located at 3 Long Grove Road, Long Grove, IL 60047. Its phone number is (312) 634-3060.

The Dog House
PARKING FOR CUSTOMERS AND BUILDING TENANTS ONLY

SHE'LL TAKE MANHATTAN

It may have been a matter of breeding—her mother, Mary Jennings Chase, owned one of the top Golden Retriever kennels in the United States—or it may have been that her first safari in 1969 awakened Lynn Chase's interest in animals. Whatever the impetus, the results are clear. Chase has become noted for her colorful paintings of animals, and she's opening a shop for chic Manhattan dogs. The walls will be studded with Chase's animal portraits, and the merchandise will include hats, leashes, harnesses, backpacks, rugged turtleneck sweaters, and Chase's own line of high-fashion attire, Bark Avenue, created and marketed in tandem with Chase's partner Marsha Feltingoff. Clothes may make the dog, but finishing touches must be added even after you've donned black tie and tails. Chase's shop will be able to lend some extra polish with information on grooming services, canine hotels, and dog sitters. You'll even be able to think of your purchase as philanthropic; Chase and Feltingoff plan to donate a percentage of the store's profits to animal conservation organizations. Feel free to bring your people. They can browse through the paintings, porcelain, china, clothing made for humans, and other gifts with animal motifs. For information on the store's exact location, now planned for Madison Avenue at 72nd Street, contact Bark Avenue at (212) 949-0918.

POWER BARKERS

It's an event like no other, a gathering of America's most celebrated and powerful dogs. It's the Kal Kan Capital Canine Follies, an annual show to benefit the Capital Children's Museum, and all Washington's barking about it.

The first Follies were held in 1985 and were presided over by the nation's first dog, Lucky Reagan. In 1986, the ousted Lucky was replaced as Honorary Petron by Rex Reagan, and although the transition from Lucky's administration to Rex's was not smooth in all respects, it was trouble-free in the case of the Follies. Rex responded immediately to an invitation from "poet, impresario, and Schnauzer" Jasper Meese, explaining that although he could not be present at the festivities, he was honored to receive the title of petron and wished the organizers well. He even signed the memo with his own pawprint.

In response to Rex's generous endorsement, Jasper commissioned interior designer Theo Hayes to build a special 5′ x 5′ x 5′ "white house" for the King Charles Cavalier Spaniel. Said Hayes of the house: "It's very colonial, the whole thing. White clapboard, with a cedar shingle roof. I didn't do it feminine or prissy. It's not as if I was doing it for a French Poodle or a Chihuahua." The conservatively styled gift seats Rex in the lap of luxury when he isn't in the lap of the First Lady. It features a parquet floor, a mailbox, red custom draperies, a window box with red geraniums, a silver bowl full of jellybeans and Milk-Bones, a down bed covered with red-white-and-blue plaid, an American Flag in the bedroom, and framed pictures of the Reagans. It was presented to Rex at the opening of the 1986 Follies; Zsa Zsa's dog, Macho Gabor, bit the ceremonial ribbon.

Judges of the Follies have included such notable humans as James Brady and Zbigniew Brzezinski. The celebrity dogs are divided into classes. Diplomatic dogs compete in the Ambassadoggerel category; sports and entertainment figures compete with other Hot Doggers. Republican and Democratic dogs square off in the Dog-Eat-Dog World competition, while Business Bow-Wows and Media Hounds get their share of attention as well. Awards for the floppiest ears, the saddest eyes, and the most beguiling bark are bestowed on gracious winners, and dogs and people alike gather information and refreshments from nearby booths.

The list of canine competitors and benefactors reads like a Washington *Who's Who.* It includes names like Kiltie Weinberger, Leader Dole, Ashley Regan, Champ Thurmond, Duke Domenici, Digger Mondale, La Coquette Udall, Harriet Basset Baker, Cokie Buchwald, Koko Iacocca, Damien Koppel, Linde Proxmire, and Blondie Theisman. Even the Marine Corps mascot, Chesty VIII, has graced the event. The Ambassadoggerel Committee is privileged by the contributions of hard-working diplomats like Bwana Kidogo. Kidogo, a Yorkshire Terrier whose name means "Mr. Little" in Swahili, chairs the committee and is rumored to have great influence with Netherlands Ambassador Richard H. Fein.

Kal Kan, the sponsor of the Follies, solicited comments from the people associated with powerful Washington dogs and published the findings in *The Kal Kan Report: Our Capital Pets.* Most of the people surveyed spend more than three hours a day with their dogs and display pictures of them at home; half take their dogs with them when they travel. One-third keep pictures of their dogs in their offices, and many celebrate canine birthdays. Often, dogs' names are closely related to their people's jobs. For example, Sheila Tate's Golden Retriever had the perfect name to match Tate's work as Nancy Reagan's Press Secretary: Misinformation.

CUTTING OUT THE COMPETITION

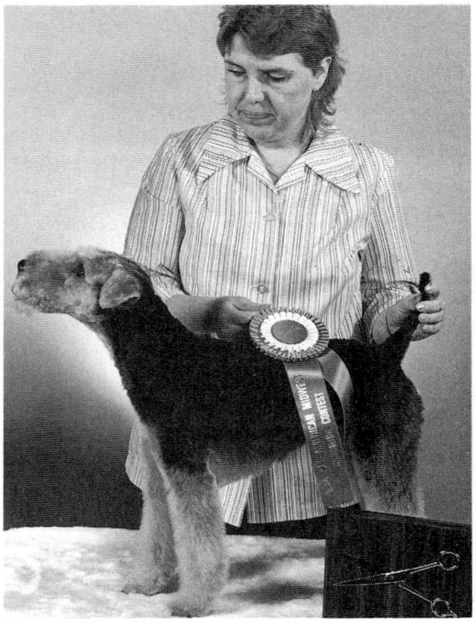

ART CRAFT PHOTOGRAPHERS

If you're anxious to look your best, brush up against some of the contestants at the All-American Midwest Professional Dog Grooming Contest. When the fur stops flying, you could be top dog; seminars as well as contests at this annual event keep groomers in perfect trim. For information, contact Jerry Schinberg, 791 Beau Dr., Des Plaines, IL 60016, (312) 364-4547.

ON THE ROAD AGAIN

The year was 1985, and something twenty feet long, eight feet wide, brown-and-white, and barking had just begun moving through New York City. No, it wasn't a giant dog. It was the dogmobile or, as it's officially named, the ASPCA Mobile Adoption Unit. Five or six days a week, dogs eager to find people of their own climb aboard. The staff on the van screens humans who apply for adoption. So far, more than one thousand dogs and cats have found homes in all five boroughs. For information contact: The American Society for the Prevention of Cruelty to Animals, 441 East 92nd Street, New York, NY 10128, (212) 876-7700.

ASPCA Mobile Adoption Unit

© ANNE DAY

GREAT LOOKS FOR GREAT DANES

Cropped ears are both classic and stylish, but sometimes we forget the sensitivity of the ears immediately after the operation. The Harrison family, shown here, has come up with the perfect device for protecting tender spots until you're all healed. Adapted from gallon milk jugs, these daring new-wave helmets can also be used for puppy's first Halloween.

CARLA HOTVEDT/SILVER IMAGE

A New Breed of Empathy

BODY AND SOUL

BEHAVIOR

Illustration from *A Dog's Life*

A Labrador Retriever is herded into the back of a station wagon for an agonizing three-hour drive. The bumps in the road, the hot afternoon sun, and the shrill voices of the children strain his nerves badly, and the uncertainty of this "adventure" stretches them almost to the breaking point. When the car finally stops, he is ushered into a room full of unfamiliar people, strange smells, and harsh noises. The humans seem to be enjoying themselves, but there's not a dog alive who can't sympathize with the Retriever. We can almost feel the rising tension, the rush of hormones, the wave of nervous energy.

Thanks to a pamphlet produced by the ALPO Center for Advanced Pet Study (P.O. Box 2187, Allentown PA 18001), humans may be able to empathize with that Retriever as well. The situation described above is one of several presented in **"A Dog's Life: Stress and Your Dog."** The pamphlet tells humans which situations we dogs may find stressful and urges them, "if you want to lighten your dog's burden of stress, learn to think like him."

This sentiment has been expressed a great deal lately, and it may be the beginning of a new era in canine-human relations. People are starting to realize that it's not enough to hand out treats once in a while. We need a little empathy as well.

One recent example of a book written in this new vein is appropriately entitled **"How to Speak Dog."** Written by Lucine Hansz Flynn, *How to Speak Dog* covers a number of classic subjects, such as housebreaking, learning new tricks, and obedience classes. Flynn stresses the importance of praise as well as firmness and consistency, and she explains not only how humans should speak and gesture to dogs but also how to interpret our sounds and movements when we talk to them. Flynn, unlike most authors, also grasps the real nature of the canine-human relationship, referring to the principal human character in her book as "the dog's lady." Furthermore, the real stars are Tasha, a Pomeranian, and Dimity, a Golden Retriever. The narrative is generally enjoyable and contains a good deal of useful information, as well as some righteous anger about the unscrupulous and irresponsible practices of some breeders and pet shops. *How to Speak Dog* can be ordered from Denlinger's Publishers, Ltd., P.O. Box 76, Fairfax, VA 22030, (703) 830-4646.

BEFORE YOU GO HOME WITH YOUR NEW DOG, STOP & GET A NYLON OR LEATHER BUCKLE-ON COLLAR (BUCKLE IT JUST TIGHT ENOUGH SO THAT HE CAN'T PULL HIS HEAD OUT), & THE LONGEST LEASH YOU CAN FIND. GET ONE MADE OF NYLON OR COTTON WEBBING, 6-10 FEET LONG IF POSSIBLE. SMALL ROPE OR PARACHUTE CORD WITH A BOLT SNAP OR SPRING SNAP TIED ON THE END WILL DO IN A PINCH. DON'T GET A CHAIN LINK LEASH & KEEP IN MIND THAT LEATHER LEASHES ARE VERY TEMPTING TO CHEW ON & EXPENSIVE TO REPLACE. ALSO GET A NYLABONE OR RAWHIDE BONE & SOME DRY DOG FOOD. DON'T LET HIM CHEW ON HIS LEASH!
NO.
HERE, CHEW THIS
GOOD DOG!
A WORD ABOUT WALKING ON LEASH—
① IF YOUR DOG WON'T MOVE, DON'T PULL HIM! BEND DOWN, COAX HIM, BE NICE, TALK SOFTLY; SAY 'GOOD DOG!' WHENEVER HE MAKES A MOVE IN THE RIGHT DIRECTION. BE PATIENT! OFFER HIM PIECES OF DOG FOOD. HE'LL MOVE EVENTUALLY. WAIT FOR HIM TO DO IT.
② IF YOUR DOG IS A PULLER, EVERY ONCE IN A WHILE PLANT YOURSELF LIKE A TREE, HANG ON TO YOUR END OF THE LEASH & WAIT. (DON'T JERK, JUST STAND & WAIT.) WHENEVER YOU FEEL ANY SLACK IN THE LEASH, SAY 'GOOD DOG!' THEN CONTINUE YOUR WALK. BE PATIENT!
✱ IF YOUR DOG HAS BEEN LIVING WITH YOU FOR A WHILE ALREADY, START HERE. PLAY WITH HIM FOR A WHILE, LET HIM GET A BIG DRINK OF WATER, PUT ON HIS LEASH, THEN HEAD FOR THE BEDROOM OR THE COUCH & SETTLE IN. YOU CAN DO THIS EVERY DAY OR ONLY ON WEEKENDS. THE MORE OFTEN YOU DO IT, THE SOONER HE'LL BE HOUSEBROKEN.
HOW ABOUT A NAP? I'LL TAKE ONE, TOO. HERE'S YOUR BONE
THIS IS BORING! I GUESS I'LL LIE DOWN & CHEW ON THIS BONE
DOWN, GOOD DOG!
TIE HIS LEASH TO THE BEDPOST OR TO A BIG SCREW EYE SET IN A WALL STUD NEAR THE FLOOR. DO THIS ONLY WHEN YOU'RE IN THE ROOM WITH HIM. YOU COULD SIT DOWN & WATCH TV OR READ. KEEP THE LEASH SHORT SO YOUR DOG GETS BORED & LIES DOWN AT YOUR FEET WITH HIS BONE. STEP ON THE LEASH SO HE WON'T BE ABLE TO CLIMB IN YOUR LAP. (IF HE'S A LAP DOG, INVITE HIM UP & SAY 'GOOD DOG!' WHEN HE HOPS UP.) HE SHOULD LIE DOWN DURING ALL OF YOUR MEALS, TOO, OUT OF THE WAY OF TRAFFIC.
LATER . . . (STILL NAPPING)
I HAVE TO GO OUT!
Wooo! oooo!
OUTSIDE? GOOD DOG!
YOUR DOG MAY SAY WUFF! OR HMMM! PAY ATTENTION! IT MIGHT NOT BE MUCH.
OKAY, LET'S GO!
HURRY UP!

Illustration from *Housebreaking*

Flynn's emphasis on praise is echoed in a brochure on housebreaking by Linnea Johnson. Everybody likes to hear some words of encouragement and appreciation now and then, and even the name of Johnson's company, **Good Dog! Dog Goods,** reflects a commitment to making dogs feel good about themselves. The brochure, in a delightful comic-book format, costs $2 and can be ordered from Linnea Johnson, Good Dog! Dog Goods, 1506 Eden Valley Road, Port Angeles, WA 98362.

Pet therapists are also becoming popular. Dr.

Nice Dimity!

Illustration from *How to Speak Dog*

BODY AND SOUL

Humans are beginning to look at the world from our point of view, and it's changing the way they treat us.

Dr. Dog as analyst and analysand.

Dennis Fetko, also known as **Dr. Dog**, has devoted years to convincing humans that a dog with a bad habit isn't all bad. He's gone to great lengths to show them our point of view, to explain how we think, and to show how humans can confuse us by training us improperly or by unconsciously reinforcing our bad habits. Dr. Dog works as an animal behaviorist in San Diego, hosts a regular radio program, has issued a series of cassettes about canine psychology, and is presently writing a book designed to help humans understand us better. For more information on Dr. Dog's methods, write: Dr. Dog, P.O. Box 28176, San Diego, CA 92128 or call: (619) 485-7433.

Another pet therapist, **Samantha Khury,** takes empathy even farther, claiming to be able to communicate with animals telepathically. "As a child," she says, "I could always communicate with animals and heal them. I could feel the energy flow from my hands." Khury's canine clients include Brutus, a Doberman featured on 'Magnum P.I." For more information, write: Samantha Khury, 610 McLain St., Escondido, CA 92027.

Animal trainers, too, are moving toward empathy and praise in their work. Trainer, pet expert, author, and conservationist **Brian Kilcommons** certainly emphasizes kindness when he trains dogs. He feels that it's important for us to enjoy learning, and his canine students, numbering over 25,000, agree. Kilcommons has had a special rapport with dogs all his life, and his work with us is not limited to that done by his company, Kilcommons Professional Dog Training, Ltd. His investigative reports for television news programs have led to a number of reforms, including the closing of a New York-area shelter which was notoriously abusive in its practices. For information on his work as a trainer, a guest lecturer, and an animal expert, contact: Brian Kilcommons, P.O. Box 887, Point Lookout, NY 11569, (212) 613-9074.

Brian Kilcommons.

If your people are getting divorced, if they don't spend enough time with you, if there's a new baby in the house and you're feeling neglected, or if you've been living so long with finicky humans that you've picked up an eating disorder, you may need the services of an animal behaviorist. **Warren Eckstein** is perhaps the best-known animal therapist in the United States, making regular or semi-regular appearances on *Hour Magazine, The CBS Morning Program,* a local San Francisco television program, and Viacom cable on Long Island. He also occasionally sets up animal stunts for *Saturday Night Live* and *Late Night With David Letterman.* Although he's treated pigs, snakes, and even a tarantula, dogs remain the largest segment of his clientele.

Dogs associated with human celebrities have also consulted Eckstein, among them Lily Tomlin's Norwich Terrier Tess, Al Pacino's mutts Lucky and Suzie, and Cheryl Tieg's Wire Fox Terrier Martini. David Letterman's dogs

arren Eckstein. BRUCE MORGAN

Bob and Stan did likewise when they had difficulty adjusting to New York. "The amazing thing about working with Letterman's dogs," says Eckstein, "is that they have the exact same personality he has. I swear, if I'd met Bob for the first time on the street, I would've known that he was Letterman's dog. He even has the space between his teeth."

Eckstein's approach stresses love rather than domination, recommending communication—praise and reprimands—instead of food or a rolled-up newspaper. He works on discovering and confronting a dog's real problem, not just addressing the symptoms. Warren and his wife, Fay, were also pioneers in pet-facilitated therapy.

Eckstein receives a great deal of mail from troubled dogs and humans, but that doesn't necessarily mean that he's too busy to help you. He's prepared several multi-page letters on common problems which can be ordered for $4.99 each. They are: "Housebreaking," "Proper Walking," "Chewing," "Sit & Stay," "Come When Called," "Car Sickness & Auto Manners," "Fear of Storms & Other Noises," "Stress and Your Pet," "Jumping on Furniture & People," "Teaching Pets to Get Along," and "Preparing the Pet for the Baby." If your particular problem doesn't fall into one of these categories, Eckstein will do his best to answer your letter free of charge. Be as specific as possible in your letters, including at least your age, what type of dog you are, and a description of your humans' lifestyle. You might also want to subscribe to "Warren Eckstein's Hugs and Kisses Newsletter," which includes nutrition and medical information, behavorial advice, answers to readers' letters, trivia, a guide to new products, Eckstein's schedule of appearances, and gossip about the dogs of the stars. A one-year subscription costs $15; two years cost $28. Warren and Fay Eckstein have also written two books. *Understanding Your Pet* can be ordered through any bookstore, and *Pet Aerobics* is available through Eckstein. Both are $16.95. For more information, or to order the newsletter or the books, contact: Warren Eckstein, P.O. Box 422, Oceanside, NY 11572, (516) 746-2683.

ASK DR. RUTH | Late-Night Advice from Dr. Ruth Weimaraner

Dr. Ruth, I have a thing about human legs. Big legs, little legs, fat legs, skinny legs, stockinged legs, bare legs. Any legs. As soon as I see them, I stand on my hind feet, grab on for dear life, and hump away for all I'm worth. My owners have had to apologize to guests for me on more than one occasion, and I've had my rear smacked until even I'm embarrassed. But to no avail. The second I see another human leg, I'm at it again. What shall I do? My owners are talking about taking drastic measures if I don't control this obsession.

Shame on your people for smacking you when you obviously need a more sensible solution to your problem. If suggesting that you need a live-in girlfriend of your own gets you nowhere, I'd recommend you try simple Freudian transference to keep your urges under control. Pretend that legs are giant vacuum cleaners or washtubs or anything else you absolutely hate. After a couple of days of such pretending, you'll soon lose interest in legs and find yourself completely cured. Just make certain that you don't pretend that legs are fireplugs or trees. That'll only get you in worse trouble.

Dr. Ruth, I'm worried. My father tells me that if I play with myself, hair will grow on my paws. I've just looked—and they're *hairy*. Help!

Stop worrying. Your father is obviously putting you on. Ask him to show you his *paws.*

Dr. Ruth, I'm getting desperate. One of the neighborhood bitches is in heat, and my owner won't let me outside. I've tried everything to call attention to my problem—and I mean *everything*. But all he gives me is a lousy fifteen minutes in the yard on a leash. What can I do?

First ask yourself—do you really care about this bitch? Are you willing to be a little patient for her sake? If the answer is yes, try a more subtle approach with your owner. Look mournfully at the door. Stare out the window and whimper. If your owner has a partner of his own, try interrupting them frequently in the bedroom. You'll be surprised at how quickly he gets the message.

Dr. Ruth, the dog I'm involved with is a really boring lover. *Really boring*. As soon as he's finished, he's gone. He runs away, plays with his toys, and forgets all about me. Every time, he ends up trotting away down the street with this smug, self-satisfied look on his face, and I end up barking after him, "That was *it*?" He never answers. He never wants to talk. And as soon as I'm out of heat, it's like I never *existed*. I could be a tree, for all he cares.

Oh, dear. Perhaps you shouldn't be barking insults at him. You could be hurting his feelings. But I think you're right. You do have a problem, and it's important to make him understand that you have needs. Sit with him and try to communicate without barking at each other. If that doesn't work, I think you should both go to a therapist.

Dr. Ruth, I'm a purebred who's won several prizes at dog shows, and I'm trying to have puppies. Unfortunately, because of my show record, my owners see my puppies as potential sources of profit. They're planning to select my mate on the basis of his heritage, and I have absolutely no say in the matter. Our criteria are completely different—they want a champion with perfect coloring and great posture, and I want someone sensitive and caring. He could be a mutt, for all I care. What should I do?

Well, the first thing that I would like to make absolutely clear *is that you do* not *have to have puppies with any dog you dislike. You can always make it perfectly obvious to your owners and to the dog in question that you have no interest in him, and your owners will eventually give up or try another dog. So you do at least have a negative voice in what's going on.*

The second point I would like to make is that it's important to give each dog a fair chance. Admittedly, you may not have all the time you'd like to get to know him, but don't assume *you won't like him. Being a champion doesn't automatically make a dog a bad lover or an insensitive beast. After all, you seem nice enough, and you've won prizes. Humans have a saying: "It's just as easy to fall in love with a rich man as a poor man." I propose that we modify that saying to read: "It's just as easy to fall in love with a purebred as a mutt."*

Next, consider how he feels. You're not the only one being put in an awkward situation. He's probably just as nervous as you are, and being honest about your feelings may put you both at ease.

Lastly, it's a good idea to think of the puppies themselves. If your owners are going to a great deal of effort to find you a suitable mate, they're also planning to find good homes for the puppies. If, instead, you find yourself a mutt—who may be a perfectly nice dog—your people may not feel so responsible for the puppies, and it may be much harder to find homes for them.

Dr. Ruth, I have to admit something. I've been doing it doggy-style all my life, and it's getting pretty dull. Aren't there any other positions?

Oh, my, yes. Humans have been experimenting with them for centuries. But I think you'd better not try them. They're almost all logistically impossible for canines. If you want to add some excitement to your sex life, there are better ways to do it than by requiring the services of a chiropractor.

Dr. Ruth, my owner yells at me whenever I lick myself, especially in front of guests. Doesn't he know that I'm just trying to keep myself clean?

Attempting to impose human mores on dogs is a sign of gross immaturity. Bark at him the next time he powders himself for jock itch. See how he *likes it.*

Health Pacemaker bank...getting the point... playing it safe...

PACING YOURSELF

A pacemaker may not be the answer to every dog's heart trouble, but for a few it can be the key to a longer, more fulfilling life. It certainly was for Linde, a Florida Schnauzer whose heart rate was more than twice as slow as it should have been. Linde was losing consciousness several times a day, but the operation was successful, and Linde once again enjoys a favorite activity—playing a toy piano. The cost of the operation was underwritten by the Pinellas Animal Foundation, which also runs the national pacemaker bank that furnished the crucial device. Donors bequeath their pacemakers to the bank or offer ones they are replacing; used pacemakers cannot be placed again in humans, but they can still save the lives of dogs. If the operation is a success, there's only a one to two week recovery period. For more information, contact: Pinellas Animal Foundation, 7533 38th Ave. North, St. Petersburg, FL 33710, (813) 347-PETS.

Aid and Comfort

Discovering that you have a terminal or cripplingly painful illness is terrifying. The thought that, at any moment, a sudden accident could result in your death is similarly chilling. But it's not the thought of death that bothers us—it's the fear that the humans we leave behind us will suffer. Current psychological opinion holds that the death of a dog can be as harrowing to our people as the death of a human friend or relative. Thanks to the ALPO Pet Center, you can help your people adjust to your death by sending for a pamphlet entitled "Death of the Family Pet: Losing a Family Friend." It explains the stages of grieving and lists sources of support and information. Write: ALPO Pet Center, ALPO Petfoods, Inc., P.O. Box 2187, Allentown, PA 18001.

Nothing But The Tooth

If you're over five years old, there's a 95% chance that you have some form of periodontal disease. Even if you're young, have a look at your mouth. Do you see inflamed or receding gums? plaque or tartar buildup? bleeding? loose, infected, or lost teeth? Do you have chronic bad breath? If the answer to any of these questions is yes, see your vet immediately. Some of the damage may be reparable; for example, your vet can remove tartar with special instruments. In between visits to the vet, you can exercise an ounce of prevention by brushing several times a week. Do not use human toothpaste, which can cause stomach complaints, or baking soda, whose high sodium content can create many problems, especially for sufferers of heart ailments. Instead, use a toothpaste designed specifically for animals, like Veterinary Prescription's C.E.T. Toothpaste or C.E.T. ProphyPaste. Both kill bacteria, produce hydrogen peroxide, help to eliminate bad breath, and have a pleasant flavor. C.E.T. Toothpaste needs no rinsing, and C.E.T. ProphyPaste has a mild abrasive to remove stubborn plaque and polish rough surfaces. Veterinary Prescription also makes a special toothbrush for dogs. Its angled handle makes it easy for your humans to use, and it has two brushes—one for small and one for large teeth. The nylon bristles are dense and are at least four times softer than the average child's toothbrush. For information on Veterinary Prescription products, see your vet.

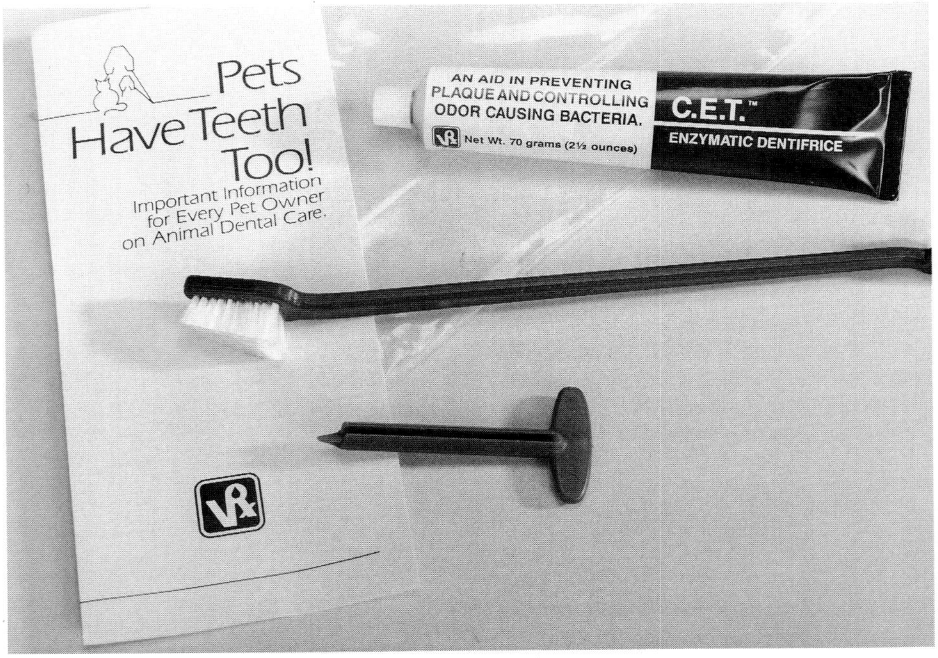
Pets Have Teeth Too!
Important Information for Every Pet Owner on Animal Dental Care.
AN AID IN PREVENTING PLAQUE AND CONTROLLING ODOR CAUSING BACTERIA.
Net Wt. 70 grams (2½ ounces)
C.E.T.™
ENZYMATIC DENTIFRICE

BRADLEY OLMAN

Sticking It to Us

After 3,500 years of experimental use on humans, it appears that acupuncture is safe for dogs. Veterinary acupuncture, derived from human acupuncture techniques that originated in the Orient, is being used by some vets to balance energy levels, diagnose illnesses, and prevent disease. Acupuncture also seems to be of use for first aid and emergencies. Treatments are given one to three times per week for four to six weeks, and positive results are often visible within a few treatments. Several methods are used to stimulate selected points, including fine needles, heat, massage, electricity, ultrasound, substance implantation, and lasers. While acupuncture is not sufficient for every ailment, it can be combined with Western veterinary practices for surprisingly effective results. For more information, contact: The International Veterinary Acupuncture Society, R.F.D. 1, Chester Springs, PA 19425, (215) 827-7742.

Your Old Kit Bag

Having the right first-aid kit in your home could save your life, so you might want to take a look at the one offered by Dan Hill Products. Designed and tested by a panel of fourteen veterinarians, it sells for about $30 and comes in a sturdy case with instructions and a 130-page *Pet First Aid Book*. The book includes 37 illustrations, 50 photographs, and 15 charts, and it stays flat when you open it—no holding it down with one paw while you try to do something more important. Written by six practicing vets, it includes information on feeding, breeding, normal temperatures, snakebite, heatstroke, poisoning, broken bones, choking, drowning, electric shock, and other important subjects. Symptoms, treatment, and how to get to a vet safely are covered thoroughly and concisely. The book can also be ordered separately from the first aid kit for about $8. The kit itself includes, among other items, 3″ gauze, 1″ tape, eye wash, blood sugar regulator, wound powder, vitamin A & D ointment, hydrogen peroxide, antidiarrheal formula, laxative, two-teaspoon oral syringe, nonsting antiseptic wipes, triple antibiotic ointment, sterile 3″ by 3″ pads, cold pack, thermometer, and bandage scissors. Refills of each item in the kit are available. To order the book or the first aid kit, write or call: Dan Hill Products, P.O. Box 14992, Orlando, FL 32857, (305) 282-6622.

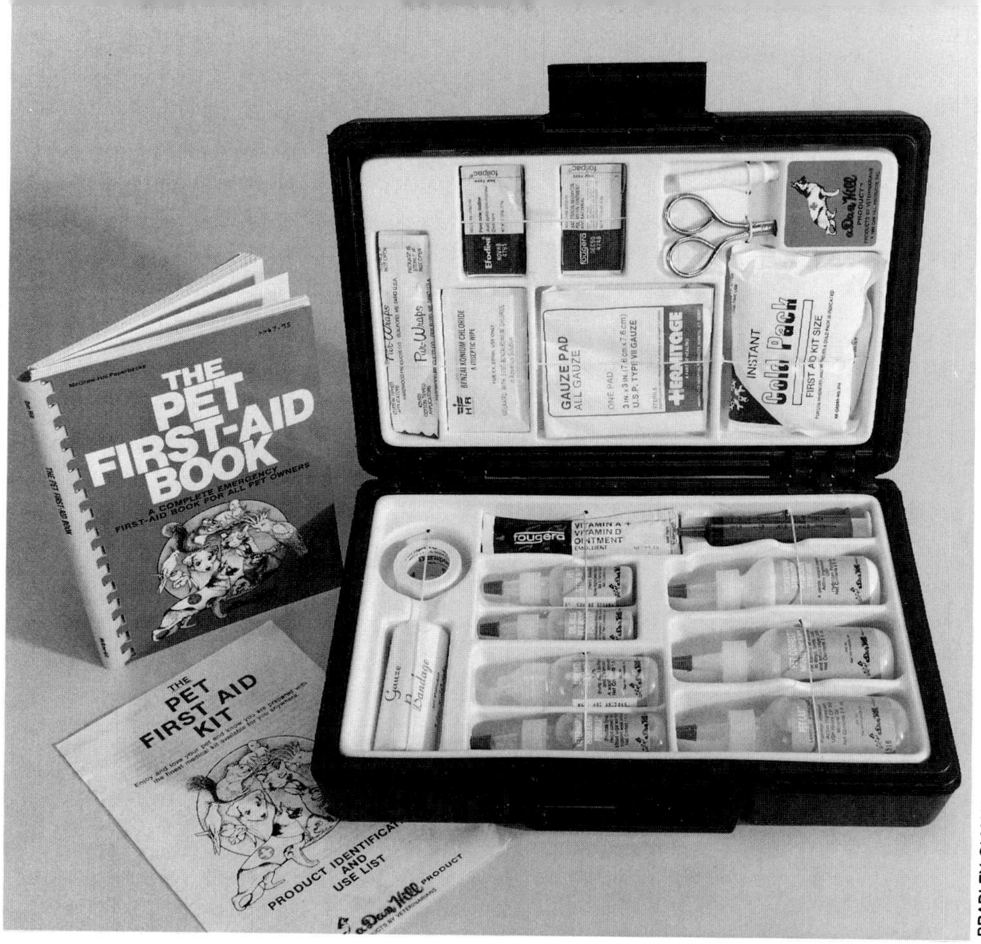
THE PET FIRST-AID BOOK
A COMPLETE EMERGENCY FIRST-AID BOOK FOR ALL PET OWNERS
THE PET FIRST AID KIT
PRODUCT IDENTIFICATION AND USE LIST
GAUZE PAD
ALL GAUZE
INSTANT
Cold Pack
VITAMIN A + VITAMIN D OINTMENT
Gauze Bandage

BRADLEY OLMAN

When Your Paws Need Refreshing

Working and hunting dogs know what rough terrain, ice, and snow can do to their pads, and any dog who's walked on salted sidewalks in the winter can sympathize. Tomlyn Products' Protecta-Pad should help. It repairs dry, cracked pads, dry, splitting nails, and elbow joint callouses, and it could be just what you need to take a step toward comfort. If you agree, ask your vet for further information.

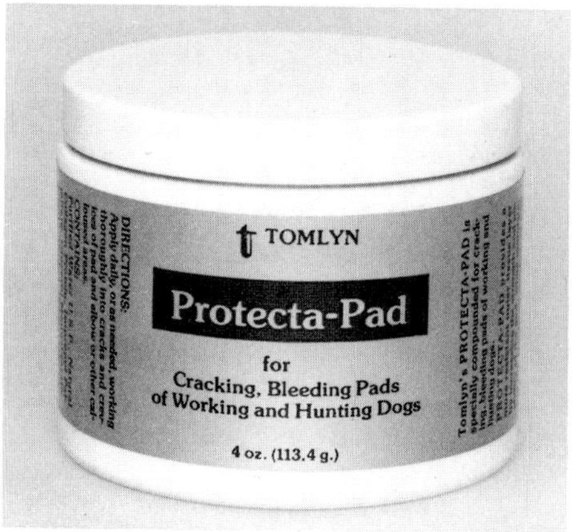
TOMLYN
Protecta-Pad
for
Cracking, Bleeding Pads
of Working and Hunting Dogs
4 oz. (113.4 g.)
DIRECTIONS

Take Coverage

POLICY #000-001
NAME: Benji
OCCUPATION: Movie Star
DOG: ☒ CAT: ☐

MULBERRY SQUARE PRODUCTIONS

About 4.5 billion dollars are spent on veterinary care every year in the United States, and veterinary costs, like human medical costs, are rising every year. However, you can keep your own expenditures lower by taking out an insurance policy. The Animal Health Insurance Agency is offering the first nationwide health and accident insurance for dogs and cats; the program is underwritten by Virginia Surety Company, Inc., and has the "exclusive and unequivocal endorsement" of the American Humane Association. The premiums are reasonable, ranging from about $36 to about $89 and making it possible for those on fixed and limited incomes to afford quality veterinary care. Dogs under ten are covered for illness and injury; those ten and over are only covered for injury. AHIA's policies do not cover elective spaying or neutering, routine checkups and vaccinations, hereditary illnesses, conditions existing before the beginning of the policy's term, whelping, cosmetic surgery, grooming, preventable diseases, mental treatment, or illness or injury resulting from coursing, racing, or commercial guarding. The company's first policy, #000-001, was issued to canine celebrity Benji. For more information, write: The Animal Health Insurance Agency, Suite 5, 24 Delay Street, Danbury, CT 06810. You can also call the company's toll-free number, 1-800-321-5400, or contact your local humane society or veterinarian.

Two happy participants in the Purina Pets for People Program.

Making "Man's Best Friend" Mean Something

by Jane Pawley

I've always found social commitment attractive. Maybe I'm nostalgic, maybe I'm naive, but it's true. There's something about a dog with a mission that compels attention and respect.

Take, for example, my friend Danny, who's involved in the **Purina Pets for People Program**. Danny, like all of the dogs and cats in the program, was down on his luck, waiting in an animal shelter for a special human to come along. Then his shelter became involved in administering the Pets for People Program.

Pets for People locates adoptable humans by making questionnaires available to people sixty years of age or older. (Interested humans can write Purina Pets for People Program, Checkerboard Square, 6T, St. Louis, MO 63164, or call this toll-free number: 1-800-345-5678. Phones are answered from 9:00 am to 4:30 pm, Central time, Monday-Friday.) The humans are required to answer questions about themselves, their housing, their ability to feed a dog or cat and provide for its health care and grooming, and the number of hours that they are generally absent from their homes. The humans who qualify for the program are then presented to appropriate dogs or cats.

Danny and his person, Bob, have become close friends. Bob, like most of the humans involved in the program, feels happier, less lonely, and safer with Danny around. Moreover, he runs fewer health risks because stroking or talking to Danny helps his blood pressure stay low and because Danny is scrupulous about taking Bob out for some exercise every day.

But it's the change in Danny that's really noticeable. Ralston-Purina gave him a new start by paying adoption fees and many initial veterinary fees. The company also provided a new leash, a collar, food and water bowls, and some food to go with them. Bob and Danny took it from there, and Danny is a new dog. He moves with confidence, knowing that he's taken on responsibility. He stands with pride, knowing that he's needed. And he plays and barks again, knowing that he's loved.

The Pinellas Animal Foundation (7533 38th Ave. North, St. Petersburg, FL 33710; telephone: 813-343-3700) and **Pets On Wheels** (1114 Cathedral Street, Baltimore, MD 21201; telephone 301-396-1762) offer similar opportunities for dogs to develop a sense of self-worth. The Pinellas Animal Foundation's Project PUP (Pets Uplifting People) sends dogs to seventy nursing homes to build humans' self-esteem, create a more home-like environment, and enhance communication and companionship. Pets On Wheels, a program of The Baltimore City Foundation and The Baltimore City Commission on Aging and Retirement Education, allows dogs with people of their own to work for a few hours a week with nursing-home residents. Dogs wishing to apply for this worthwhile program must be certified healthy by a veterinarian, pass a temperament test to make sure that they are suited for volunteer work, and readily allow handling by unfamiliar people. Dogs who qualify commit to the program for at least six months and are accompanied on their visits by human volunteers.

A similar program which screens, cares for, and integrates companion animals into nursing homes is run by the **Council on Pet Assisted Therapy**. For information on the Council's work in the New York metropolitan area, write to: P.O. Box 8003, F.D.R. Station, New York, NY 10150, or call (212) 535-3917.

Some of the noblest, most altruistic, and most attractive dogs that I've met, however, did not specialize in assisting senior citizens. Some were Seeing Eye dogs; others were members of a less well-known breed—the Hearing Ear dogs.

DAVID CRANDALL

Pets on Wheels's Taffy visits a Baltimore friend.

Dogs for the Deaf's Hearing Ear dogs, like Purina's Pets for People, are selected from the most underprivileged and downtrodden class of dogs: the dogs in Humane Society shelters, desperate for homes and for affection. Perhaps it is their knowledge of desperation that makes these talented and generous dogs so appealingly sensitive. Mingling competence and devotion, pride and obedience, Hearing Ear dogs alert deaf and severely hearing-impaired humans to noises like those of doorbells, oven timers, tea kettles, crying children, alarm clocks, smoke alarms, and telephones (TTYs). A medical committee selects people whose needs are great and can be met well by a dog's assistance. The humans are also interviewed, and those who qualify for the program are awarded to their dogs about a year after the application process begins.

Dogs for the Deaf offers a number of benefits to any dog, but especially to the small or medium-sized mixed breed who might otherwise have trouble finding a home or fulfilling work. The humans selected for the program must pro-

Dogs for the Deaf's Frank on duty.

vide a fenced yard or portable dog run, medical care, grooming, in-home training sessions to keep the volunteer's skills at their peak efficiency, and a household in which the Hearing Ear dog is the only dog. The program also allows dogs to do a little traveling, since it sends them throughout the United States. Frank, a hard-working, handsome Dachshund cross, was sent from Oregon to Athens, Georgia, to meet his person, Julie Shrader. When a dog is matched with his new owner, both dog and trainer spend a week introducing the dog to his new home. For a dog who passes the initial aptitude tests at the animal shelter, Dogs for the Deaf offers many fringe benefits, among the best of which are a good home and a new sense of confidence and importance. (Interested dogs can contact: Dogs for the Deaf, Inc., 13260 Hwy. 238, Jacksonville, OR 97530, 503-899-7177, TTY: 846-6783. Your people will not be charged in any way for your services.)

Canine Companions for Independence offers several options for Labrador Retrievers, Golden Retrievers, Doberman Pinschers, Smooth-Coated Collies, Border Collies, German Shepherds, Standard Poodles, Pembroke Welsh Corgis, Schipperkes, and Belgian Sheepdogs.

Yuppie puppies are passé. It's *in* to be altruistic.

Selected puppies of these breeds are placed in private foster homes at about eight weeks old. For the next nine to fifteen months, they are tested repeatedly for traits that will make them valuable companions; they must be loving, responsive, intelligent, in top physical condition, responsible, and hard-working. If they make the grade, they go into training for four to six months, either at the main training center in Santa Rosa, California, or at one of the branch training centers in Southern California and New York. (For more information, write: Canine Companions for Independence, P.O. Box 446, Santa Rosa, CA 95402-0446 or call: 707-528-0830.)

Dogs at Canine Companions for Independence are not merely helpful; they're specialists. Service dogs assist the physically challenged by picking up dropped objects, pushing elevator buttons, carrying items in a special backpack, turning on and off light switches, passing money to cashiers, and even selecting books from shelves. They understand at least eighty-nine commands. Signal dogs assist the deaf and severely hearing impaired. Social dogs serve as companions to individuals or institutions such as schools or convalescent hospitals. Specialty dogs are trained to help senior citizens, those with multiple disabilities, or other people with special needs. All the dogs give their humans confidence and courage. In many cases, physically challenged people find it easier to talk to others because the service dog becomes (understandably) a subject of admiring conversation, and the human's disability becomes less of a social barrier.

Founded in 1975 by Bonita Bergin, Canine Companions for Independence accepts applications only from humans wishing to be adopted, not from their relatives, friends, or colleagues, unless the human in question is a young child or intellectually incapable of filing the application. For group care facilities, the administrator makes the application. Every application must be accompanied by a $25 fee. During the second phase of the adoption process, the human visits

CCI's Ivy lends a nose.

CANINE COMPANIONS FOR INDEPENDENCE

CCI for a personal interview, unless such a visit is financially or physically impossible.

Humans approved for the program are placed on a waiting list and pre-register for a training course. About a month before the course begins, they pay a fee of $100, which includes supplies for their dog like a specially designed backpack. The two-week class has been named "boot camp" by its graduates, and it lives up to the name, demanding hard work from dogs and humans alike. At graduation, each dog usually gets to introduce the two most important humans in his life: his puppy-raiser and his new owner.

Dogs have adopted people as young as six years of age through CCI, and the program has taken them to new homes in Canada, Holland, and Israel, as well as the United States. At retirement, dogs may stay with their people or return to their puppy-raisers, living in either case a life of well-earned leisure.

The pride that CCI dogs exude may be due to their knowledge that the program has been praised by President Reagan and Surgeon General C. Everett Coop. It may come from the fact that CCI received a Distinguished Service Award

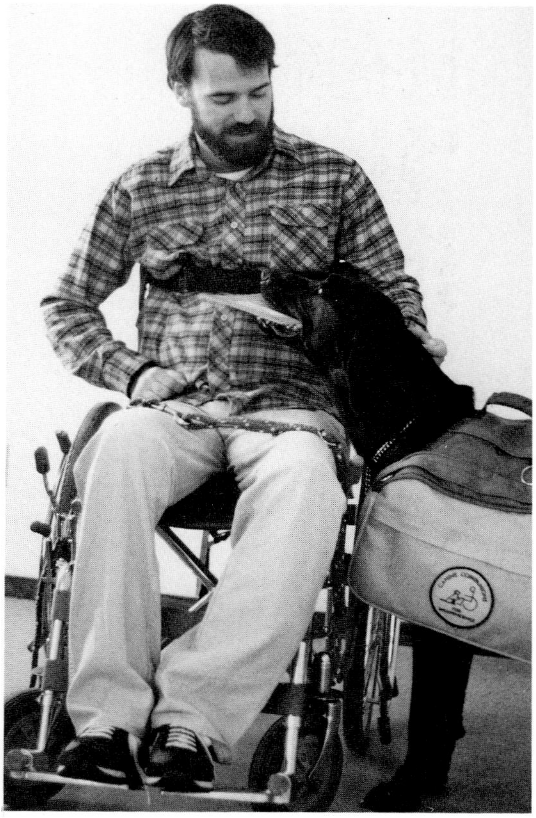

CCI dogs use brains and brawn.

from The President's Committee on Employment of the Handicapped. Or it may be that they know how much their people love and need them.

All I know is that there is something special about dogs serving mankind. Call it pride—call it dignity—call it confidence. I call it wonderful. ■

Jane Pawley is co-host of the nation's most popular morning bark show.

SNIFF IT OUT

ANNOUNCING ARAMUTT COLOGNE FOR LONG-HAIRED STUDS.

The scent is classic. Its power and sophistication are pure Aramutt. And now it's specially formulated for longer hair. It's the same perfect fragrance, but now it's just for you.

aramutt
spray cologne

INTRODUCING

ARAMUTT COLOGNE

FOR AFTER BATH,

AFTER SHAVE,

AFTER ANYTHING.

SPUDS MACKENZIE'S STYLE IS SIZZLING HOT. HE'S DASHING IN A DINNER JACKET, DOWN-HOME IN DENIM, AND SEXY IN A SWIMSUIT. . . . ON THE NEXT PAGES, YOU'LL LEARN WHAT MADE SPUDS A LEGEND AND GET A LOOK AT SOME OF THIS PARTY ANIMAL'S FAVORITE CLOTHES, INCLUDING HIS FAMOUS HAWAIIAN BEACH TOGS. FOR HOT HAWAIIAN CLOTHES LIKE SPUDS', CONTACT: DEE PET PRODUCTS, P.O. BOX 199, ARGYLE, TX 76226, (817) 464-7706.

SPUDS AND DUDS

BUD LIGHT'S MACHO PARTY ANIMAL TELLS *CQ* HOW HE MADE IT TO THE TOP. WE'LL SHOW YOU HOW AMERICA'S NEWEST SUPERSTAR SPENDS HIS DAYS, AND HOW CORPORATE SUCCESS AND PUBLIC ADULATION HAVEN'T SPOILED HIS CHARMING SIMPLICITY. HE'S NOT IN IT FOR THE FAME, HE'S JUST TRYING TO HELP PEOPLE HAVE SOME FUN.

★ ★ SUCCESS ★

Spuds MacKenzie's isn't the only success story in this issue of *CQ*. From two-time Iditarod winner Granite to Lucky Dog's Ike, dogs are making it big, and we're celebrating their achievements. And with success comes a certain sartorial flair, a sense of style, a knowledge of the rules of fashion and when to break them. We emulate their good taste, bringing you classic sweaters and the return of the hat, as well as the devil-may-care flash and glitter of an avant-garde London boutique. We'll also introduce you to some dogs who've proven that style and success don't preclude sympathy and social conscience. From Hollywood idols to hard-working civil servants, dogs everywhere are committing themselves to a new breed of dedication and service. You'll meet heroes who risked their lives to save humans or other animals, visitors to nursing homes and hospitals who enrich and prolong the lives of senior citizens and convalescents, and loyal companions who assist the handicapped by performing a startling variety of tasks. To help you join in this fashionable return to altruism, we've also suggested some gift ideas for your favorite humans. Even if you never get the chance to be a hero, you can show that you care—and we'll show you how.

THE STYLE OF THE ACHIEVERS: DOGDOM AT ITS BEST

COVER STORY

Spuds MacKenzie, the enigmatic symbol of all that's fun, grants a rare interview and allows us to glimpse the individual behind the legend . . .

By Gay Taleash

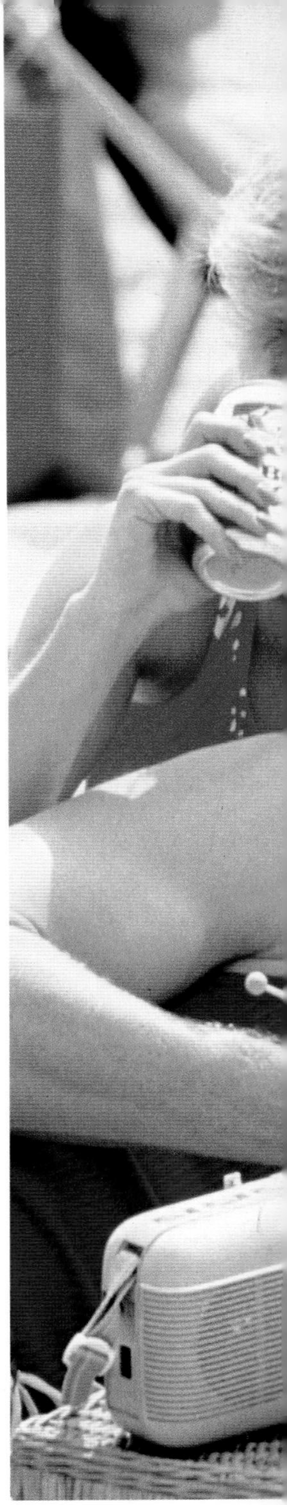

As Senior Party Consultant for Bud Light, Spuds MacKenzie travels the globe seeking out new and different ways to be the life of the party. It's a good job. But it isn't easy.

He is *the* "Original Bud Light Party Animal," a jet-set executive constantly surrounded by beautiful women, an enigma, a symbol of all that's fun. He's known the world over for his smooth style, his sharp wit, his charming and sophisticated ways. He's in constant demand as a party guest in the highest social circles.

He hobnobs with big wigs, traveling in the fast lane on a social track leading to more good times in a day than most screen idols experience in a lifetime. He's no stranger to royalty. The rich and famous beg for his counsel and advice.

But Spuds MacKenzie is not some "Good Time Charlie." To Spuds, partying is a complex mixture of science and art. And he's the pioneer

GO, SPUDS, GO

BUD LIGHT

in the field... He's the social virtuoso who can play a crowded room like a Stradivarius. And despite his fame and fortune, Spuds remains humble...

"I was just born with a talent for having fun," he said in a rare private moment recently. "And I'd be doing it even if I wasn't being paid. The guys who run Bud Light decided it was a talent I should share with the world."

The light-speed rise to Super Star status for Spuds MacKenzie began in 1983, when he met an Anheuser-Busch executive at a party. The executive (who prefers anonymity) was obviously not enjoying himself... until he met the forty-seven-pound philosopher.

Spuds shared with that man his thoughts on life and the pursuit of happiness. "One of the main ingredients in the formula for enjoying yourself is Bud Light," Spuds said. His words struck a chord with the executive and he was invited to address a board meeting at the company's St. Louis headquarters.

With Spuds for Bud, it's a dog's light with real bite. . . .

"Fun is essential to a complete life... And everyone needs to have some at the right times and in a proper way," he told the board. "But in today's world, people get so busy, sometimes they forget how easy it is. Somebody must remind them."

He got the first standing ovation ever seen in that board room (there have been several since), and a star was born.

Company executives, led by the Bud Light brand management team, decided that Spuds was right, that the world needed more happy people, and that Spuds's philosophy must be spread. They knew it couldn't be done overnight.

Spuds was immediately contracted to design and pose for posters in which he, "The Original Party Animal," would demonstrate some of his various techniques for having a good time. Contemporary adults were the first to jump on the Spuds funwagon.

But new strategies were needed to spread the word further. The next step was a calendar. It gradually caught on and people began to hang them—without shame or fear of recrimination—in offices and all manner of public places. And throughout the country, wherever Spuds's picture appeared, smiles became the rule rather than the exception.

Then came television advertising, which began in California and gradually spread until Spuds decided it was time to tell his story to the nation. He made his national debut in the Super Bowl broadcast of 1987. There are now over two hundred licensed products which bear his image, including beach towels, beer mugs, T-shirts, and watches. In fact, major department stores, among them the May Company and Macy's, have opened Spuds shops to handle the rising demand for MacKenzie merchandise.

Spuds MacKenzie now holds the executive position of Senior Party Consultant for Bud Light beer. His office at One Busch Place in St. Louis is spacious and tastefully decorated with priceless works of poster art.

When not attending parties, lunching with the stars, yachting, or sunbathing, Spuds lives in a lavish condominium at the Anheuser-Busch brewery complex in St. Louis, where he is the "philosopher of fun in-residence." He has a full staff of assistants, and he needs every one of them. In recent months, Spuds has become a media darling and a popular hero. The price of fame is a great deal of time spent on the road, making personal appearances throughout America and being interviewed on such television programs as "Good Morning America," "Today," "The Late Show," and "P.M. Magazine." In addition, Spuds is currently working on several new "Party Animal" projects. He regularly shuttles to Hollywood for the production of Bud Light commercials in which he stars and is in demand for various other film projects as well.

Although his busy social calendar and professional research and consultation duties take up the majority of his time, Spuds's private life is important to him. When his schedule permits, he lives quietly in his condo.

"It's limited, but my private time is quality time," says Spuds.

Although he has no declared or official political affiliation, Spuds often says, "I'm in favor of all parties."

His other interests include classic films of the 1930s—1939 being his favorite year. In literature and music, Spuds's tastes are varied. He often quotes the literary classics, but confesses a love for mysteries. His taste in music covers the spectrum from Mozart to Springsteen.

The Beach Boys are a particular favorite. "If it's done well, I like all kinds of music," he often says.

Spuds reveals little about his life prior to joining the Bud Light brand team, although he will concede that he spent many years as a globe-trotting "citizen of the world." No one knows his exact age, and he skillfully changes the topic of conversation when asked. When pressed for an answer, he likes to say that "Fun knows no age... but does have a legal minimum."

Although he is fluent in several languages, by preference he speaks only in a little-known language which consists of facial expressions understood only by true Party Animals. The language evolved from necessity. It originated as a form of communication among true Party Animals who spend much of their time in clubs and at parties where music volume is high and time to converse is limited.

To the uninitiated, a brief facial expression is seemingly meaningless. But in reality, a simple wink or arching of an eyebrow in the proper combination and sequence can be translated into as much as 200 words of English.

The language is catching on quickly in the multilingual cosmopolitan capitals of the world, such as Monte Carlo,

From television star to screen idol (*above*): Spuds takes time out from work on his first feature film, "Rented Lips," to confer with co-stars Martin Mull and Dick Shawn. Traveling in style (*right*): nothing but the best will do when you've reached the top.

ΔΟΓ

BUD LIGHT
BEER
BUD LIGHT
BUD LIGHT
BUD LIGHT

HOMECOM
QUEEN
B.D.O.C.
BUD LIGHT
I ♥ SPUDS
BUD LIGHT
I ♥ SPUDS
I ♥ SPUDS
BUD LIGHT
I ♥ SPUDS

"I was just born with a talent for having fun," says Spuds (*left*). And, we might add, a positive talent for attracting beautiful women (*above*).

where jet-setters have learned the value of being able to communicate articulately using only a look across a crowded casino.

Whenever Spuds travels, he is accompanied by a translator, generally another member of the Bud Light brand team. Even though some of his translators are not true Party Animals, they have learned to understand the language through close, daily association with Spuds.

As the announcer so aptly tells us in Spuds's latest TV spot for Bud Light, Spuds is "one party-lovin', happenin' dude." ■

Gay Taleash is the author of Thy Neighbor's Woof.

dressing to please your bride

it's the little things that matter most, like never stealing kibble from her dish, never taking the warmest spot by the fire or the coolest place on the kitchen floor, and letting her play with your favorite toy now and then. dressing well is important too; it shows you care enough to look your best for her.

__I do__. . . . *Opposite page*, wedding ensembles start you off in style. For him, gray moiré taffeta morning coat with black brocade trim and lace cuffs, separate white shirt trimmed with lace, black satin tie, and black moiré taffeta trousers with suspenders. Matching black top hat available. For her, white satin gown with high Victorian neck, bow at bustle, long train, and pearl and lace trimming. Matching full-length lace-trimmed veil has white organza flower appliqués and a crown of flowers attached to the headpiece.

__The honeymooners__. . . . *Above*, traditional navy-and-white cotton kimono with batik chiffon sash. On her, hair bow, feather boa, and traditional kimono in a flower print on Japanese crepe with pink silk lining and matching green and gold obi. *Left*, Saville Row blazers make traveling a snap with easy-to-fasten velcro strips. Made of imported British wool flannel in navy with red lining, epaulettes on the shoulders for a military look, and back pockets with scarves that match the lining.

__When the honeymoon is over__. . . . *Right*, four-legged rainsuits with snaps, detachable hoods, and nipped waists for a fashionable fit. Perfect for stormy weather or stormy arguments; the water-repellent surface will keep you dry when she throws her water bowl at you. All fashions illustrated here and many more are by Lynn Chase for Bark Avenue. For information, contact: Marsha Feitingoff, Bark Avenue Ltd., 300 E. 40th Street, Suite 26A, New York, NY 10016 (212) 949-0918.

PHOTOGRAPHS BY BRADLEY OLMAN

HATS ARE BACK

They've been saying so for

ears; this time they may just be righ

Opposite page: Return of an early twentieth-century tradition—the English bowler. This page (clockwise from upper left): Faux fur cap for those who care to be environmentally correct; oversize French beret—best with unconstructed jacket and baggy trousers—takes a young approach to the classics with big, easy shapes; Yellow slicker Sou'easterner for good looks in the fiercest gale; floppy felt hat for the

The Beagle Brigade and the Coyote Corps

WHERE'S THE BEEF?

by John Gregory Dane

Even in government work, there's more to success than a three-piece suit, the right collar, and a firm pawshake. The country's power elite don't all sit in the hallowed halls of Congress, behind the fences of 1600 Pennsylvania Avenue, or at the Pentagon. Two groups of unsung government employees have pawed their way to the top in recent years without the aid of pin-stripes or Poochi shoes. These canny canines have made it through a combination of hard work and expertise, without fanfare and tail waving. And they're not even members of the sexier dog professions, like drug or criminal detection. But their work is no less important and saves the government, and the taxpayers, millions of dollars a year.

The U.S. Department of Agriculture's Beagle Brigade performs a vital function at the country's bustling international airports. Since mere humans don't always understand the dangers inherent in contraband food—for example, just one orange, smuggled in undetected, could result in a dread citrus disease that would wipe out thousands of acres of groves—the beagles have been specially trained to sniff out forbidden foreign goodies. The canine pros can even detect an Italian sausage hidden in a can of tobacco. These quiet, unassuming dogs were especially chosen for their acute noses and their loving natures. Because they aren't threatening to the passengers, they can wander around the baggage carousels with impunity, carefully checking each and every bag coming off an international flight and signalling when they suspect there's contraband inside. The Beagle Brigade's success rate is running at about eighty percent—surely nothing to sniff about.

Equally successful at a very different occupation are representatives of three unusual breeds—Great Pyrenees, Hungarian Komondor, and Turkish Akbash—employed by the U.S.D.A. at its experimental sheep station in Dubois, Idaho. Chosen because they are temperamentally suited to guard dog work, and for their intimidating sizes (adults weigh in at 100 pounds or more), these stalwart citizens are sent to live with the sheep as small puppies (six to eight weeks of age). This "social bonding" generally results in firm friendships between dogs and sheep, and it isn't long before the adult dogs are on patrol, deterring the attacks of the coyotes who are the flocks' most dangerous and prevalent enemies. Wildlife biologist Jeff Green, who runs the program, placed more than sixty dogs with local ranchers as part of a seven-year test. Needless to say, the test was hugely successful, the attrition rate of most flocks was greatly reduced, and Green's dogs are now permanently on watch at sheep ranches throughout the West. ■

On his hind legs, novelist John Gregory Dane stands almost seven feet tall.

USDA-APHIS PHOTO

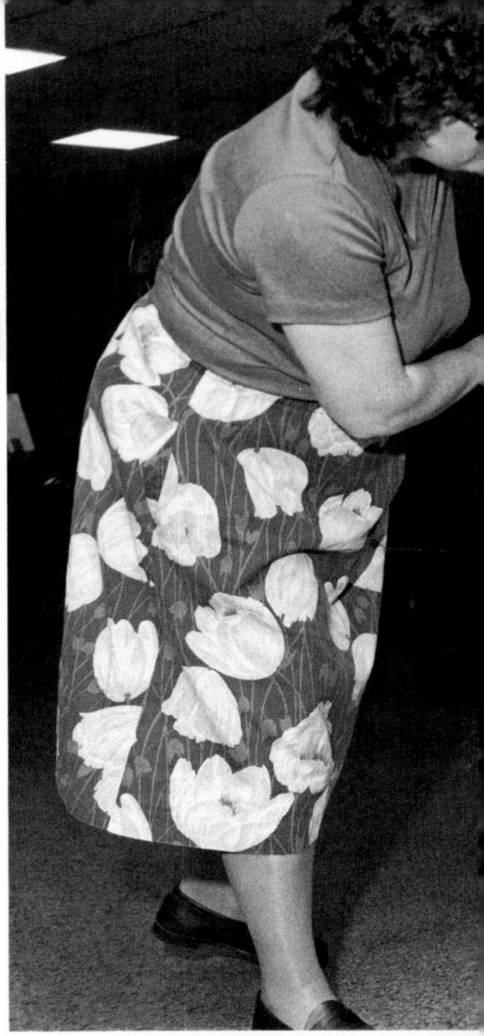

USDA PHOTO

PROTECTING
US
AGRICULTURE

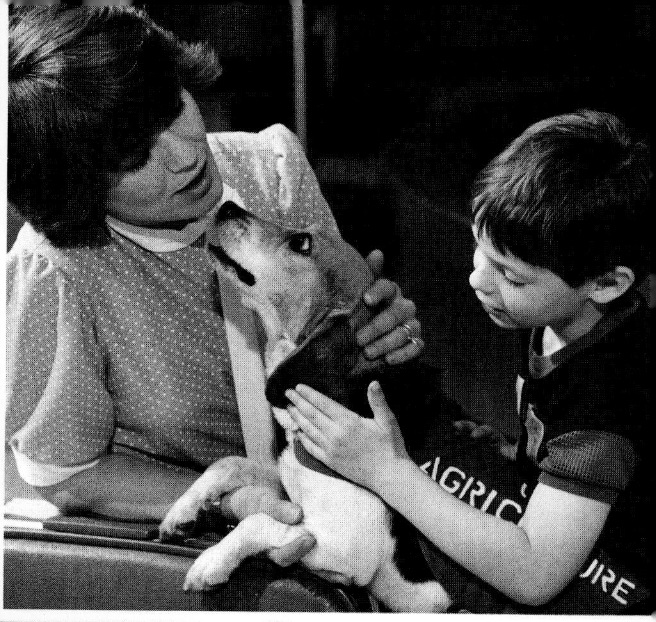

USDA-APHIS PHOTO

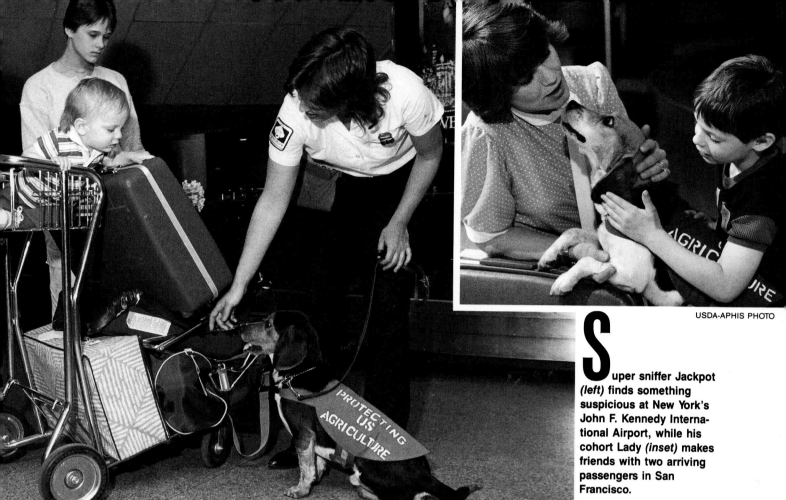

Super sniffer Jackpot *(left)* finds something suspicious at New York's John F. Kennedy International Airport, while his cohort Lady *(inset)* makes friends with two arriving passengers in San Francisco.

USDA PHOTO

A vigilant Akbash *(left)* is ever on the alert in the midst of an Idaho flock. One of his woolly Komondor compatriots *(inset)* is barely distinguishable from the sheep he protects.

GET SMART

How's your style I.Q.? Are your ties too wide or too narrow? Do your collars miss the point? If so, you've got some boning up to do. Matriculate at Petsmarts for a Ph.D. in classic canine toggery.

WITH PETSMARTS

A matched set (*opposite page*): for her, British Tan rain cape with hood over matching wrap skirt with roomy pockets—stylish rainy day coverage. For him, matching reversible raincoat (also in navy and red) with plaid lining. Called the Xtendable-Xpandable, the coat can be lengthened from one to three inches by resetting the shoulderpiece on ingenious hidden Velcro strips. (To keep you bone dry, Petsmarts also features a line of drench coats in power colors of waterproof vinyl or cotton broadcloth with sheer vinyl overliners.)

Summer coolers (*right*): thirsty cotton terry cooling coats to beat the heat on the steamiest days. In white, of course (it's the sun-reflective color), to be drenched before donning or spritzed afterwards. Beige cotton edging adds contrast, Velcro around neck and chest insures perfect fit, and three-position belt carrier guarantees comfort, no matter your musculature.

PHOTOGRAPHS BY
ROGER APPLEBY

I've got
DogSmarts

I've got
DogSmarts

Magna cum laude machismo

Best of show (*at left, top*): Before you enter the ring, that last touch-up will go much faster if you let your groomer wear this ultra-professional apron. Features include lots of pockets for all your curries and powders . . . which can travel to and from the show in a capacious canvas tote. (Our model, Held, is carrying the handsome tote, more than likely crammed with his blue ribbons.)

Brainy bulletin: why not announce your above-average intellect? For casual wear, the Petsmarts Tee (and a coordinated sweatshirt for her, if you think she's earned it). Both of easy care poly-cotton that springs back wash after wash. These and other Petsmarts fashions and accessories, singular for their sophisticated styling and subtle detailing, will keep you at the head of the class. At better boutiques, or to order from Petsmarts Inc., 225 W. 35th Street, New York, NY 10001; (212) 947-5740.

GET SIRIUS
Hollywood's Top Dog Stars

By Rona Basset

I remember, many years ago, my people took me to a drive-in movie to see *For the Love of Benji.* I was deeply impressed by Benji's talent, but I was also just a puppy, with a puppy's youthful enthusiasm. I remember thinking, as I sat in the darkened car, "That's not so hard. *I* could do that."

Well, I'm a lot older now—how *much* older I won't say—and I've learned quite a bit about the entertainment industry since then. And I know that, although they make it look easy, canine actors work hard to perfect their craft. Only those dogs with unusual skill, dedication, and charisma make it to the top.

The top, since 1951, has been represented by the PATSY (Performing Animal Top Stars of the Year) awards. The PATSYs are sponsored by the American Humane Association, which works to stop "cruelty, neglect, abuse, and exploitation of children and animals" through education, supervision of the entertainment industry, and legislation. The awards were originally designed to honor film actors only, but now animals appearing on television and in commercials are eligible as well.

The names of the PATSY winners are stirringly evocative. Asta. Benji. Lassie. Sandy. A pack of memories of unforgettable performances races through the mind. And although the lives of these actors may have been transformed by luck, it was hard work that made them stars and consummate skill that made them legends.

Take Asta, for example. His real name was Skippy, and he came to Hollywood without a bone to his name. His breed already put him at a disadvantage; trainers said that Wire-Haired Terriers were "too feisty" for the movies. But, luckily for Skippy and for all of us, trainers Henry East and Rudd Weatherwax believed in him. They believed in his expressive, black-rimmed eyes, his intelligence, and his sophisticated charm. They gave him his chance.

Their belief paid off. In 1934, Skippy landed the role of Asta in *The Thin Man,* and thus began a career which included five more *Thin Man* films with William Powell and Myrna Loy and roles in *Bringing Up Baby* and *Topper Takes a Trip.* Skippy was paid ten times the normal salary for canine actors during the Depression. But it wasn't his luck or his wealth that his co-stars remembered; it was his dedication to his art. Constant practice

BENJI

Benji makes his debut as cinematographer. Action! Camera! Roll 'em!

enabled him to learn new tricks in as little as two days, and Powell and Loy were both impressed by their colleague's professionalism.

Similarly, the original Benji, whose real name was Higgins, got a boost from luck and then made the most of it through diligent effort. As a puppy, Higgins sat in an animal shelter looking for love, or at least for a way out of his pen. He found both in trainer Frank Inn, who gave him a home and acting lessons. Higgins soon became familiar to American television audiences as the star of "Petticoat Junction," which ran from 1963 to 1970. Such a career would have made any dog happy, but there was more to come. In 1974, at the age of 13, Higgins crowned a lifetime of achievement with his performance in *Benji*, drawing critical acclaim for his emotional range and skilled stunt work.

Sandy was another refugee from an animal shelter. Discovered the day before he was to be put to sleep, Sandy became the first dog in the history of Broadway to do a scene alone. The Broadway Sandy (as opposed to the nine road-company Sandys and understudies or the movie Sandy, who was played by an Otterhound named Bingo) played his part from 1977 to 1983, has been to the White House six times, and received the American Humane Association's Craven Award for outstanding stunt work in 1978.

How do you get to the PATSY awards? Practice, practice, practice.

But the spirit of the PATSYs has always been represented by Lassie. The dogs who have played her—all of them male, all trained by Rudd Weatherwax, and all descendants of Pal, the original Lassie, have won eight first or second-place PATSYs. The movies and television series about Lassie spanned thirty-five years, and generations of dogs know her familiar whimper and bark as well as they know their own. Here, too, luck was partially responsible for the creation of a star. Pal, the original portrayer of Lassie, was brought to Weatherwax as an eight-month-old, "untrainable" puppy. After Weatherwax cured the puppy of his bad habits, he was allowed to keep Pal in lieu of payment for the training. Some acting lessons and a lot of hard work later, Pal auditioned for the lead role in *Lassie Come Home* (1943), but he was only chosen as a stand-in. In true Hollywood style, Pal's performance as a stand-in was so spectacular that the director changed his mind, and Pal became the first Lassie.

Of course, not every Patsy winner is still a doghousehold word, and some actors revered today for their contributions never received PATSYs. John Javna, who has worked variously as a street musician, a balloon-selling clown, a gold mine caretaker, and a toy manufacturer, and who is now a historian of pop culture, has written a book which celebrates *Animal Superstars* of all species. Javna includes many canine PATSY winners, but he also writes about dogs whose careers had ended before the award was established, legendary actors who were never given the honor, and dogs who were stars in their day but have been forgotten in ours. Filled with amusing gossip, inside information, vital statistics, and photographs, *Animal Superstars* barks about Cleo, the Basset Hound coached by Frank Inn, Benji's trainer. Noted for her sarcastic humor, Cleo starred on "The People's Choice" with Jackie Cooper and could fall over backwards, arch her back and bark like a seal, and stand on her head in a corner.

Also included in *Animal Superstars* is Buck, the St. Bernard who was launched to fame by *The Call of the Wild* (1931) and driven to an early and tragic death by the dog-eat-dog competition of Hollywood. Although no one was ever charged with Buck's murder, he died of poisoning at a time when he and several other dogs were rivals for a role in a Darryl F. Zanuck film.

Javna's book alerts us to new faces, like that of Mike, a Scottish Border Collie whose performance as Matisse in *Down and Out in Beverly Hills* (1986) brought him instant fame. *Animal Superstars* also pays tribute to some of the first canine stars: to Pete, co-star of dozens of *Our Gang* movies between 1927 and 1938; to Terry, the Cairn Terrier who played Toto in *The Wizard of Oz* (1939); and to Rin-Tin-Tin, played by four German Shepherds who took Rinty from1920s silents to 1950s television. Rinty saved damsels from distress and Warner Brothers Studios from bankruptcy; he was insured for $250,000 and had a personal bodyguard of five dogs and a mansion across the street from Jean Harlow's.

We must remember, however, that for each of the dogs who appears in *Animal Superstars,* there are thousands who hunted for stardom and failed. Desire and a repertoire of standard tricks are not enough. An actor needs an implicit trust in the trainer, even when it seems that a stunt is dangerous, and an ability to concentrate intently on the script, even with cameras, lights, and a crew around. Canine superstars are never content with ordinary tricks, or even with maintaining a stock of particularly clever or difficult ones. They cultivate versatility and daring, always learning new stunts, new techniques, and new expressions. As Carmelita Pope, head of the American Humane Assocation's Hollywood office, writes in her introduction to Javna's *Animal Superstars,* "Any well-trained animal can be a good actor. But to become a star, an animal has to be extraordinary, with the same appeal and charisma that a human star has."

To find out more about animals who have had that "appeal and charisma," you can order *Animal Superstars* by contacting Hal Leonard Books, 8112 Bluemound Rd., P.O. Box 13819, Milwaukee, WI 53213, (414) 774-3630. For more information on the PATSY awards or on the important work being done by the American Humane Association, contact the Association at 14144 Ventura Blvd., Sherman Oaks, CA 91423, (818) 501-0123. ■

Rona Basset's voice has recently been declared a national monument.

Clockwise from upper left: **Sammy's Shadow ("The Shaggy Dog") and Asta accept their PATSYs (1960); television's Rin-Tin-Tin is made beautiful for a take; Nick Nolte and Mike in "Down and Out in Beverly Hills"; Lassie, inducted into the American Humane Association's Hall of Fame in 1973.**

AMERICAN HUMANE ASSOCIATION

ANIMAL SUPERSTARS
BY JOHN JAVNA
BENJI
FRED
MIKE
BEN

AMERICAN HUMANE ASSOCIATION

PUTTIN' ON

London's poshest boutique sets the stage for fashions that are positively post-punk. . . .

THE GLITZ

Britain's posh puppies and punk pooches have been hunting for fashion they can get their teeth into. And they've found it—at Kahniverous. Jane Kahn, M.A., and her partner, Tokky the Tart, design and sell ahead-of-their-time clothes for men, women, dogs, and cats "who dare to be adventurous." Winter or summer, day or evening, the Kahnivour style—flash, splash, and dash—gets you noticed. Attention is the key—Kahn grabs it with fur, feathers, leather, sequins, leopard skin, lamé, satin, or zebra stripes—whatever it takes to make you different from the rest of the pack.

Begging for attention. . . . *Opposite page*, designer Jane Kahn with Lord Binty's dog Barnie, who steals the scene in a Kaprie coat with silver saddle, stirrup detail, and feathered collar. *This page*, the cutting edge of fashion trims classics down to a dog's size. . . . *Above*, Barnie in a Barbor country coat with tartan wool lining and scarf. *Below*, Barnie in a Cavalier coat with lace collar and diamante trims on embroidered velvet. All by Kahniverous, c/o Hyper Hyper, 26-40 Kensington High Street, London, England W8, 01-937-4480 or 609-7880.

BRUSHUPS & COMB-OUTS

Messy doesn't mean macho. Well-groomed Shepherds and stylish Samoyeds alike know the importance of sleek fur, well-trimmed nails, and an attractive scent. So should you.

First things first: lather up with House of An-ju's cocoa butter and mink oil shampoo (especially good for long coats) or Sulfodene Medicated Shampoo to combat itching and hot spots. For stubborn snarls, finish with Hagen's Balsam Conditioner Cream Rinse. After you shake dry, remaining tangles will melt with a Resco coarse comb. Then shape the perfect look with a Mason Pearson nylon and bristle brush (*in travel kit*) or a Richter all-nylon one. House of Hindes's rubber-backed curry is just the thing for a special massage. Hold and Style Spray from Town & Country Dogs will maintain your just-groomed perfection. (Between shampoos, try Cherrybrook's Grooming powder to absorb excess oil.) Pedicures are a snap with Classic Products Nail Clippers and a Pet-i-cure Diamon Deb file. Final touches: Vitacoat's Diamondeye to remove stubborn tear stains, Bio-Groom's Groom 'n Fresh Cologne for an elegant spritz of scent, and a Theralin VMP vitamin every day to maintain that shiny perfection from within. Special grooming tips for your particular needs are outlined in Arco's *All-Breed Dog Grooming Guide*.

House of An-ju
Cocoa Butter & Mink Oil Shampoo
HAGEN
BALSAM CONDITIONER
CREAM RINSE
SUPER CONCENTRATE
ECONOMY SIZE
Sulfodene
MEDICATED
Cherrybrook
GROOMING POWDER
FOR ALL BREEDS
NET WT. 10 OZ
CHERRYBROOK
BOX 15
Town & Country Dogs
HOLD AND STYLE SPRAY
200 ml.
Vitacoat
DIAMONDEYE
Groom 'n Fresh
BIO-GROOM
Theralin
VMP TABLETS
THE ALL BRE
DOG
GROOM
GUI

Jr. Charitable Trust.
BIO-GROOM®
Spray Set™
Coat Texturizer
Gives coat extra hold and texture, but leaves hair with natural feel
NET 16 FL. OZ. (480 m
BIO-GROOM
Coat Polish
Four Paws
K-zyme
Canine Nutritional Supplement
Chewable Tablets
100 TABLETS
GOLD BOND
SINCE 1908
MEDICATED
POWDER
Opticlear™ II
SOOTHING EYE SOLUTION
DECONGESTANT
STERILE
Net Contents 4 fl oz (118 ml)
PARIS
NEW YORK
Cologne For Pets
Rodeo Drive Fragrance Collection
by CARDINAL
Lambert Kay
Ear-Rite
Insecticidal Ear Wash for Dogs
Aids in Wax Removal
Controls Ear Mites
Lovely Breath
60 TABLETS

Feeling good is critical: start with K-zyme chewable tablets for supplementary nutrients. Then use Ear-Rite insecticidal wash to remove wax and control mites. Opticlear II Eye Solution has a soothing decongestant to clear up red, swollen, or teary eyes. Finally, get relief from chafing, prickly heat, insect bites, and other skin irritations with Gold Bond Medicated Powder. Once you're feeling great, concentrate on looking great. Give your coat shine and tangle-free manageability with Four Paws Soft 'n Silky or Bio-Groom's Spray Set or Coat Polish. Classic Products' tempered steel scissors offer a lifetime of styling ease, and the Carnaby Club boar bristle brush makes the most of whatever cut you choose. The last step is smelling great with Lovely Breath and the Rodeo Drive Fragrance Collection, which includes three powerful scents—Beverly Hills, New York, and Paris. All of the products illustrated on these pages, except the Rodeo Drive Fragrance Collection, are included in the Cherrybrook catalogue, which features the largest collection of canine supplies in North America. For a free copy, call or write: Cherrybrook, Route 57, Box 15, Broadway, NJ 08808, (800) 524-0820. In New Jersey, call: (201) 689-7979. For information on the Rodeo Drive Fragrances, contact: Cardinal Laboratories, 710 S. Ayon Ave., Ayusa, CA 91702, (818) 969-3305.

PULLOVER PIZAZZ

Let it snow, let it snow, let it snow. Warm sweaters will keep you comfortable when the mercury falls and ready for any occasion that rises.

BRADLEY OLMAN

This season brings a kennelful of traditional favorites reworked in bright colors and striking patterns. They're perfect for skiing, sledding, Christmas parties, long walks in the snow, and evenings out.

All there in black and white. . . . *Opposite page,* Bichon Boo Boo and Westie Keegan in all-wool outfits by Karen's for People and Pets. On Boo Boo, "Hexagon Baseball" sweater and matching beret. On Keegan, red-accented geometric sweater and matching checkered cap.

Off the rack. . . . *This page,* wool and wool-blend hand-knit sweaters in vivid colors and daring styles. Brand-new classics include a knit tuxedo to wear to the Borzoi Ballet and a pack of argyles, better than ever in bold new colors. All hand-knit and all by Karen's for People and Pets, 1220 Lexington Ave., New York, NY 10028, (212) 472-9440.

BRADLEY OLMAN

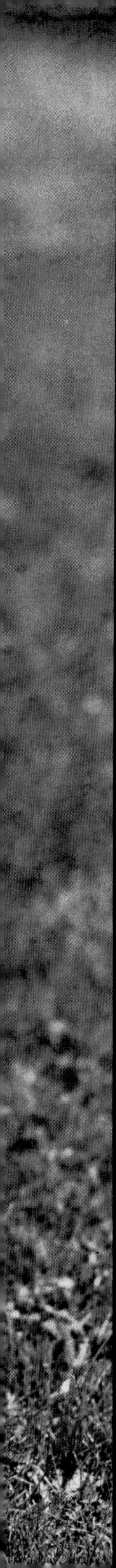

PULLOVER PIZAZZ

BRADLEY OLMAN

OHIO
STATE

Oh, give me a bone. . . . *Opposite page,* red bulk-knit acrylic sweater with a bone motif, by Ben Richter Designs. Available at better pet shops in sizes 10 to 20; other colors include green, royal blue, and fuchsia. **Win one for the Yipper**. . . . *This page, top,* "College Classics" sweater in school colors, available in sizes 10, 12, 14, 16, and 18/20, about $22. Sizes 22, 24, 26, about $25. Embroidered letters may also read "Washington Huskies," "Oklahoma Sooners," "Michigan Go Blue," "NEBRASKA," "Pitt Panthers," or "Penn State"; other schools may be added if enough requests are received. By Pampered Pet, 1007 East Third Street, Williamsport, PA 17701, (717) 323-4383. **Hit the slopes**. . . . *Bottom,* acrylic snowflake sweaters for fitting in without blending in, from Pedigrees, 15 Turner Drive, Spencerport, NY 14559, (716) 352-1232. Sizes 10, 12, 14, 16, and 18, about $14. Sizes 20, 22, and 24, about $15. Available in black with red snowflakes or red with gray.

PULLOVER PIZAZZ

© RAEANNE RUBENSTEIN, 1987 TELEPHOTO

Bright, bold, and brilliant. . . . *This page,* all-wool geometric-patterned "Fortune 500" sweater. On her, a matching hand-knit human version. Both by Karen's for People and Pets, 1220 Lexington Ave., New York, NY 10028, (212) 472-9440. Karen's is the most fashionable canine salon in fashionable New York. Come in and let Karen Thompson groom and dress you to perfection and beyond.

Designed to go with your favorite whine. . . . "Formal Wear" argyle sweater in silver and gold metallic yarn on a black body, sizes 8 to 18 and 20 to 24; navy "Ritz" oversized vest with yellow hearts and yellow and off-white details, sizes 8 to 18; and "Varsity" turtleneck in royal blue, red, and white, sizes 10 to 20. These 100% acrylic, double jacquard-knit sweaters and many others are available from Doggiduds, 160 E. 38th Street, Box 221, New York, NY 10016, (212) 692-9226.

12

From Mutt With Moxie to Famous Fido

BY WILLIAM F. BARKLEY, JR.

LATE ON THE NIGHT OF OCTOBER 20, 1984, Texas police officer Dave Koschel is on patrol with his partner Zeus, a German Shepherd/Alsatian cross. They spot a car theft suspect. When the suspect ignores Koschel's order to halt, Zeus attacks, and a .357 caliber bullet slams into the dog's left shoulder, knocking him off his feet and hurling him several feet away. Undaunted, he leaps at the gunman's arm just as a second shot at point-blank range is aimed at Officer Koschel. Instead of wounding Koschel fatally, the bullet is deflected and hits his leg. Zeus chases the suspect away and guards Koschel until help arrives.

Every dog is special, but some, like Zeus, are especially brave and get the opportunity to display their courage and devotion. Some North American organizations, including the Texas Veterinary Medical Association (TVMA) and the makers of Ken-L Ration dog food, have made an effort to recognize the heroes among us.

Zeus was inducted into the TVMA Pet Hall of Fame in August, 1985. Both he and Officer Koschel had recovered from their wounds, and the gunman who shot them had been apprehended. Between the time of the shooting and his death in February, 1986, Zeus assisted in the capture of 106 felons. After Zeus's death, the TVMA donated $1000 toward the training of Austin, Koschel's new canine partner.

The TVMA Hall of Fame was established in 1984 "to honor animals who, through unselfish or courageous accomplishment, exemplify the human/animal bond." Other recipients include Duke, a Labrador Retriever, and Prince, a Miniature Poodle, both of whom rescued their owners from burning houses; Pooch, a mixed breed, who ran for help when farmer Pleas Fortune was pinned under a tractor; and Leo, a Standard Poodle. Leo defended eleven-year-old Sean Callahan from a five-foot rattlesnake by jumping between Sean and the snake. Struck six times in the head and left eyelid before retreating, Leo bought enough time to allow Sean to get away and to allow Sean's father, Bud, to shoot the rattler. Leo was rushed to a veterinarian's clinic; his head swelled so quickly on the way that Sean's mother, Lana, had to cut off his collar. The vet who cared for Leo feared that Leo would die, suffer brain damage, or lose his left eye.

Leo accepts his plaque as a member of the TVMA Hall of Fame.

Zeus rests on his laurels.

Today, Leo is alive, alert, and using both his eyes.

Leo also received the Ken-L Ration Dog Hero of the Year Award. Potential dog heroes are selected from reports in the media, nominations by local officials, and suggestions from the general public. A panel then chooses finalists, and any dog or person can vote for the ultimate winner.

The first dog hero was chosen in 1954. Tang was a Collie from Denison, Texas, who saved children from being struck by cars on five different occasions. Since then, twenty-one male and thirteen female dogs from twenty-two states and of mixed heritage and twelve breeds have been honored. Ken-L Ration dog heroes receive a medal, a year's supply of dog food, and national recognition. Many of the winners have rescued humans from drowning, burning, or attack by other animals. One winner even rescued 300 goats from a fire.

A few feats of heroism spotlighted by the Ken-L Ration program are particularly notable. In 1956, Lassie, a Sheltie from San Carlos, California, was watching her owners' six-year-old son, who had just undergone surgery. Lassie noticed that something was wrong and alerted her owners, who found that the boy was hemorrhaging badly.

The 1970 award went to a St. Bernard of surpassing courage. The Denali, Alaska, dog saved his owner from an attacking grizzly bear. Woodie, a mixed breed, won the award in 1980, for leaping from an 80-foot cliff to save a drowning man.

The competition was particularly stiff in 1986. There were six finalists: Frankie, who saved a human from being trampled by a horse; Buddy Ben, who saved his owners from a tornado which crushed their motor home; Tiger, who found help after his owner was injured by a buck and stranded on an isolated logging road; Fritz von Weaven, who saved a diabetic by warming him with his body and barking for help; and the winners, Champ and Buddy. Champ, a seven-year-old Cairn Terrier, and Buddy, a three-year-old mixed breed, are the first dogs ever to share the award. At 2:30 a.m., battling a temperature of twenty degrees below zero, they discovered a man trapped under a 2,680-pound piece of machinery. They summoned help and saved him from dying of shock.

Champ and Buddy.

Buddy Ben.

If you would like to nominate a friend for Ken-L Ration's Dog Hero of the Year Award, write: Dog Hero of the Year, 231 South Green Street, P.O. Box PET, Chicago, IL 60607. If your nominee lives in Texas, he or she is also eligible for the TVMA Hall of Fame. Nomination forms must be signed by the nominee's owner and a member of the TVMA. Contact: Texas Veterinary Medical Association, 6633 Highway 290 East, Suite 201, Austin, TX 78723, (512) 452-4224. ■

William F. Barkley, Jr., enjoys writing, howling on moonlit nights, and hunting liberals.

GIFTS FOR YOUR FAVORITE HUMAN

DOGUE
woof
a parody of the world's most famous fashion magazine
best bets for bow-wows
the pick of the designer collections:
puppy ellis
canine klein
ruff lauren
beauty bonus:
grrreat grrrooming and magical makeovers

If you're padding the floor night after night, scratching your ear in bewilderment over just *what* to give that very special person in your life for that very special occasion, take heart. *CQ*'s editors have scoured the continent in search of presents guaranteed to bring you pats aplenty—and lots of extra goodies off your owner's dinner plate. We've suggested gifts for large and small people, both male and female. Best of all, each will be a daily reminder of faithful, thoughtful you!

ROLL OVER VOGUE

Chic, glitzy, filled with irresistible fashion photographs by such canine shutterbugs as Fido Scavullo and Houndmutt Newton, *Dogue* is great fun—a brilliant parody of haute couture for the haute canine. Bone up on the glamorous togs of Yves Saint Bernard, Canine Klein, and Ruff Lauren. Order a copy for your person and one for that special woman in your life. At just $8.95 a copy (plus $1.50 postage and handling), it's a doggone steal. Write The Main Street Press, William Case House, Pittstown, NJ 08867.

RAIN, RAIN, DON'T GO AWAY

Why would you want the rain to stop, when you and your two-legged companion can take your walk sheltered under this sophisticated paw-print umbrella? In black-on-white or white-on-black with sleek wood handle. At better boutiques, or from Petworthies Ltd., 4 Brookside Place, Westport, CT 06880; (203) 227-0187.

BRADLEY OLMAN

A Howling Good Cause

Determined Productions makes these cuddly plush animals (*opposite page*) and equips each one with its own brush and an owner's manual full of helpful tips for humans on the care of their living pets. Best of all, a portion of the sale price of each fluffy feline and canine goes to aid the fine work of the Humane Society of the United States. Available at your favorite gift or department store, or contact: Determined Gift, P.O. Box 2150, San Francisco, CA 94126, (415) 433-0660.

GIFTS

STAY BETWEEN THE LINES

Need a perfect stocking stuffer or no-occasion present for your favorite small person? The folks at ALPO have just the ticket. Their coloring book, *You and Your Puppy,* has lots of lively illustrations to challenge budding artists. Best of all, its helpful suggestions will teach them how to treat *you* properly. And it's free. Write ALPO Pet Center, P.O. Box 2187, Allentown, PA 18001.

YAPPY BIRTHDAY

Once you've chosen the perfect present, you'll want the perfect card to go with it. And it's never easy to find a card that expresses just how you feel. But several companies understand your special needs and have attempted to give you a good range of greetings to choose from. One such is Argus Communications, whose Quotable Critters Collection, in particular, has some terrific selections for birthdays, anniversaries, and no-occasions (if your person's away on a long trip, for instance, you might want to send a card just to say you miss him).

Pawprints dog cards feature the clever illustrations of Wallace Tripp and Janetta Lewis, among other artists. Tripp's version of *American Gothic* (an anniversary card) is a particular favorite of ours. Pawprints and Argus cards are available at stationery shops everywhere, as are Pawprints colorful gift wrappings (featuring pawprints, of course).

At Christmas time, you'll find Diebold Designs' cards particularly enticing; the messages are tailor made for you ("Happy Howlidays" and "Bark the Herald Angels Sing" are just two) and the colorful cartoons bring special cheer. Diebold cards can be ordered imprinted, if your card list is a long one. Write the company at High Bridge Road, Lyme, NH 03768, or call (603) 795-4592 for its latest catalog.

Who misses you?
Happy Birthday!
You still have the body of a young pup.

Cards from Pawprints (*top*) and Argus (*middle and bottom*) for all occasions.

Unwelcome Mat

If your family is constantly dogged by uninvited visitors, Poly Enterprises offers a potential deterrent. Its intimidating door mat features a snarling shepherd and the threat: "Go Ahead. Make His Day." The slogan "Dog on Property" can be replaced with any one of a variety of stock messages, or you can order the mat personalized with your owner's name—or yours. Measuring 19" by 30", the mat is made of tough rubberized vinyl. Order it for $19.95 (plus $3. shipping) from Poly Enterprises, 230 E. Pomona Ave., Monrovia, CA 91016, (818) 358-5115.

For further emphasis, throw in some "Warning! Bad Dog" stickers from Four Paws Products. The black, red, and white stickers measure a convenient 3" by 4", making them ideal for windowpanes, doors, and other small areas. Four Paws makes a variety of stickers and larger (6" by 9" and 9" by 12") aluminum warning signs; they are available at shops across the country.

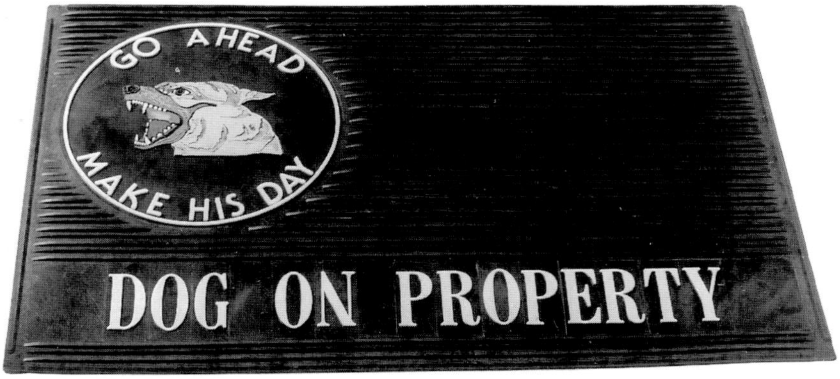
GO AHEAD
MAKE HIS DAY
DOG ON PROPERTY

CHECK IT OUT

Lighten his bill-paying burden (and make him forget your latest vet bill) by ordering customized checks for him. . .checks with your picture on them. To place your order, send one of your person's current checks (voided), a deposit slip, and $7.50 for each 200 checks ordered, to Kansas Bank Note Company, P.O. Box 360, Fredonia, KS 66736. Allow three weeks for delivery. The company has 140 different dog illustrations in stock. Every purebred is included, of course, and there's even a mixed breed. For an extra $20 you can have your own inimitable self printed on the checks. Just send a favorite photo along with your order.

SPECIAL DELIVERY

If there's a philatelist in the family, request a selection of stamp sets on approval from Taylor and Company, P.O. Box 1075, Dept. D, Calgary, Alberta, Canada T2P 2K4. Enclose $1.00 with your approval request, and you'll receive a 20-page illustrated booklet on stamp collecting. Taylor specializes in—what else?—postage issues featuring man's best friend. Dogs as faithful companions, heroes, workers, rescuers, and even space travelers are depicted on an amazing range of stamps from around the world. The company can't honor requests for individual breeds, no matter how special you think you are. But the variety of full-color stamps it offers is truly amazing. Once you've looked over the selection of sets Taylor will send on request, purchase those that have particular appeal and return the rest.

GUARANTEED GENUINE
POSTAGE STAMPS OF THE WORLD
PRICE: $2.49

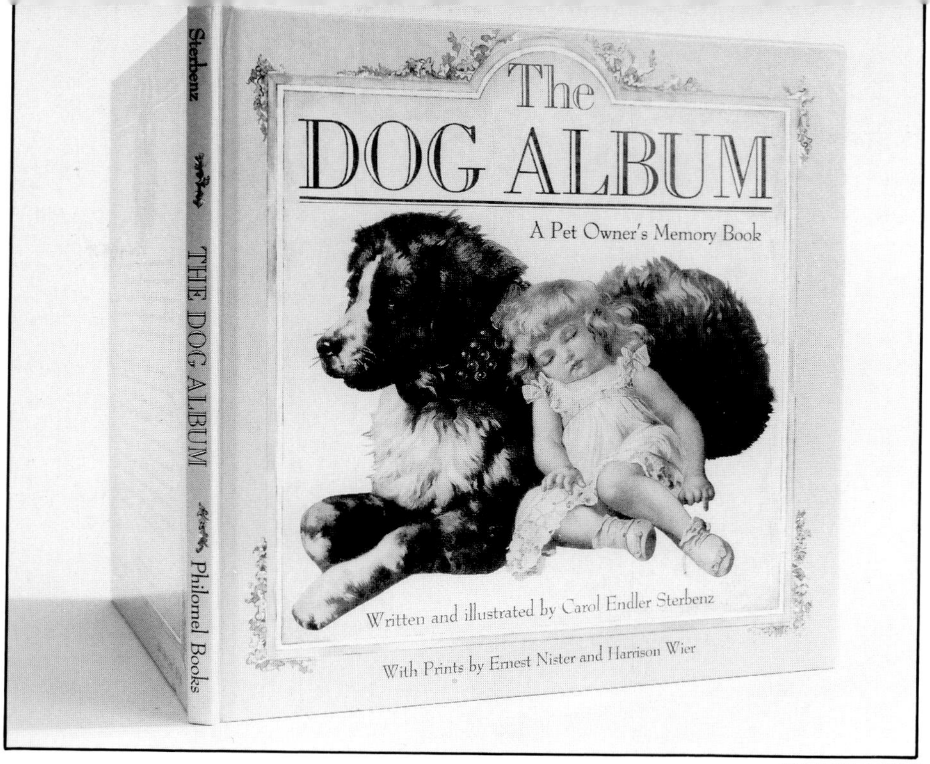
Sterbenz
THE DOG ALBUM
Philomel Books
The DOG ALBUM
A Pet Owner's Memory Book
Written and illustrated by Carol Endler Sterbenz
With Prints by Ernest Nister and Harrison Wier

BRADLEY OLMAN

THINGS THAT YOU DO

Memories Are Made of These

Chances are that your owners are forever taking pictures of you—especially when you're being particularly engaging (which, of course, is all the time). And it's likely that those Kodachromes wind up tucked in all sorts of obscure places where they might never again see the light of day. To avoid that sorry possibility, give your people a useful gift which will get them organized *and* provide a permanent record of you. *The Dog Album*, chock-full of lush Victorian illustrations in full color, has space for photos, health and vaccination records, dog sitter's instructions, and even an official Adoption Certificate to prove your special place in the family. Published by Philomel Books, it is $11.95 at bookstores. *My Memories*, another choice, is a spiral-bound records and photo album with 32 pages of charming color illustrations that accompany your personal commentary on matters such as vaccinations, house-training, favorite foods, travel, and ancestry. Eight large pocket-pages provide ample space to store medical records, breeding papers, diplomas, and other certificates. $7 at pet shops, or contact The Hot-Z Company, P.O. Box 66, Morrison, MO 65061. (314) 486-2210.

(If you have a special photo of yourself that deserves special treatment, look for a Famous Fido's Foto Friends display at your local pet shop. Famous Fido will take your negative, slide, or print, size it to your order, and mount it permanently on quarter-inch white acrylic, then cut it to outline your shapely shape. Standard sizes are 3 by 5 or 4 by 6 ($14.95), 5 by 7 ($19.95), or 8 by 10 ($24.95). Larger sizes can be made to your custom order. The result will be a striking sculpture of you destined for pride of place on your person's mantel or end table. For further information, contact Famous Fido's Foto Friends. 1533 West Devon Ave., Chicago, IL 60660. (312) 761-6029.

GIFTS

DOGMA
TRIVIA GAME
FOR DOG LOVERS

BRADLEY OLMAN

Twenty Questions Plus

Your humans are probably fond of telling you that they understand the meaning of your every bark and whine, not to mention the centuries of breeding that make you behave as you do. Test their perceptions and their perspicacity with this clever trivia game. Dogma includes 53 plastic-coated question/answer cards containing a total of 350 questions, some of which are guaranteed to puzzle 'em. A pewter paw-printed die regulates the play. $9.95, from Paws 'n Shop.

CARRY ON

PML

BRADLEY OLMAN

Why let your person carry an ordinary tote bag when you can order one with your handsome likeness embroidered on it? Shown at left, Paws 'n Shop's roomy tote measures 13½″ wide by 10½″ high by 4″ deep. The company makes it in combinations of red and navy, tan and navy, or in solid navy, and of heavy-duty Cordura strong enough to hold all your toys and trappings *and* some of the paraphernalia humans feel compelled to lug along. Embroidery includes a name or initials and your choice of one of 79 AKC-recognized breeds. Two inner zippered pockets are perfect for keeping your biscuits or other treats close at hand. Each, $39.95.

Paws 'n Shop's Bermuda bag (*right*) has a sleekly finished, removable hardwood handle. Also available in red, navy, or beige Cordura with contrasting trim, it is fully lined and comes with the same wide selection of eye-catching canine embroidery. Each, $24.95. (Both Paws 'n Shop bags can also be had with a number of kitty likenesses, just in case you need to prove your unswerving loyalty to that unwelcome but ever-present housemate. . . .)

HAVING ALL THE MARBLES

One of the most personal presents you can give is a likeness of you in oils or in clay. If your wallet won't stretch that far, these cold-cast marble figurines (*opposite page*) would be the next best thing. Dozens of different breeds are captured in amazing lifelikeness. (If you were born on the wrong side of the dog blanket, there's even a handsome mutt.) Sizes vary according to individual breed, from 1½″ to 5½″ in height and 2″ to 6″ in length. Each, $39.95, from Paws 'n Shop.

The more I see
of mankind
the more I like
my dog
Dogs are God's
way of smiling
at the world
Me

GOT THE MESSAGE?

You are unique, and obviously irreplaceable. It might not be a bad idea to give the other members of your household a subtle reminder of your sterling qualities, and if the message is artfully embroidered on comfy decorator pillows, so much the better. Exclusively from Paws 'n Shop, these washable polyester-stuffed pillows are covered in beige or navy washable linen with contrasting binding and measure 14″ square. Choose any of the statements illustrated. Each, $19.95.

Pam and Bob Luby of Paws 'n Shop have a special understanding of your needs—and those of your people. In addition to the lovely items featured on these two pages, they carry countless other perfect gifts for humans—and also for you. Their colorful direct-mail catalog is a must for the dog—or dog-owner—on a shopping spree. To get the latest one, write Paws 'n Shop, 23 Birchwood Circle, Bedford, NH 03102, or call (603) 622-0544.

HAUTE CUISINE

By Craig Clawborne

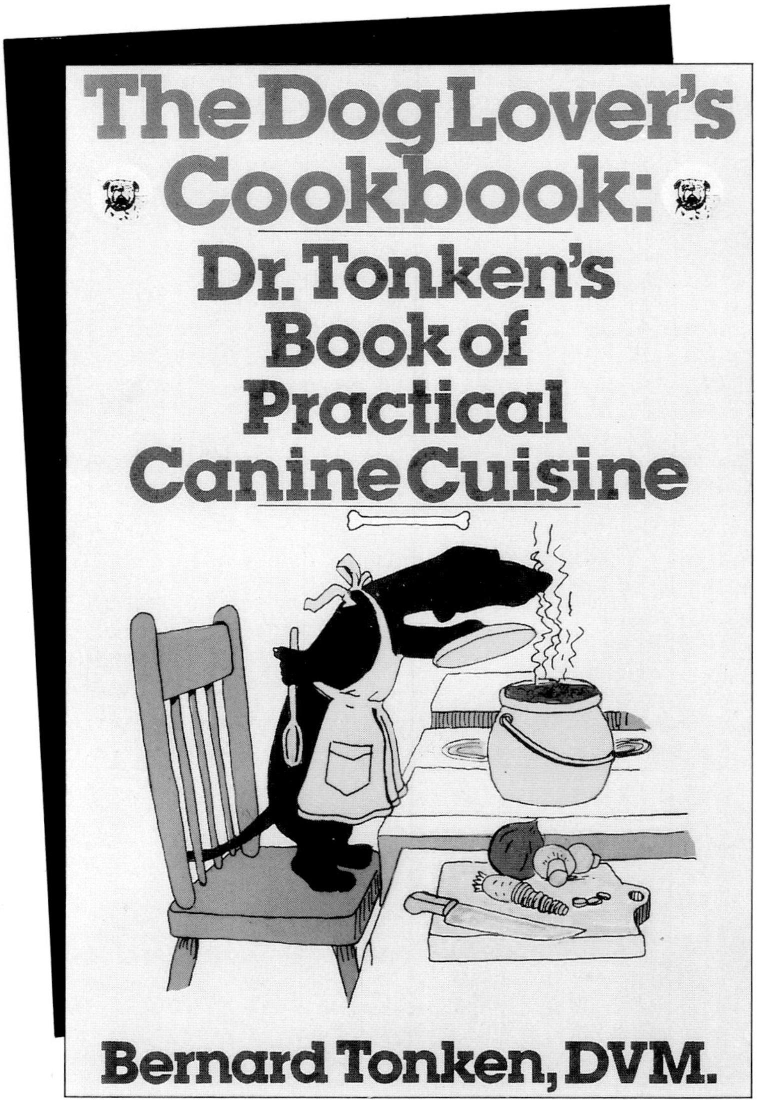
The Dog Lover's Cookbook:
Dr. Tonken's Book of Practical Canine Cuisine
Bernard Tonken, DVM.

Dr. Tonken's entrees will make you sit up and beg for more

A Book of Practical, Delicious Meals is Waiting to End Your Ennui

The typical dog's diet is about as exciting as watching your nails grow. The flavor or texture of the food may change slightly if you're lucky, but it's pretty much the same thing, day after day after day. Let's face it—when your owners are saying, "Oh, boy, isn't this yummy? This looks sooo good!" you *know* they don't mean it. After all, have they ever given up a sandwich, a steak, or bacon and eggs to try a little of *your* food?

You may not be able to entice your humans away from their favorite foods, but you can get them to vary your diet and tailor it to your individual needs. *The Dog Lover's Cookbook,* by noted Canadian veterinarian Bernard Tonken, will give them plenty of information on dogs' nutritional requirements and plenty of mouth-watering recipes. Also included are dishes designed for the special needs of sick, overweight, working, pregnant, and very young dogs. All the recipes, including those printed below, have been taste-tested and approved by Farrah, Dr. Tonken's German Shepherd-Coyote cross.

Just leave these recipes around for your owners to find:

MIXED VEGETABLE SOUP

This economical broth is made by using:

1 small onion
2 stalks celery
2 medium-sized carrots
1 medium-sized parsnip
¼ cup barley

Add all ingredients to a pot containing 1 quart of water. Salt to taste.

Bring to a boil and simmer for 1 hour.

Allow to cool to warm, and serve.

Vegetables may be strained off and mixed with other foods.

Freeze excess broth for future use.

BACON 'N EGGS BREADED

"For You Or Your Owner"

Fry 3 slices of bacon to a crisp and then chop.

Mix the bacon with ½ cup of soft bread crumbs.

ILLUSTRATIONS BY DON INMAN

Leave the drippings from the bacon in the pan and add the bread crumbs mix to it. Heat until crumbs are crisp and brown. Remove from pan.

Mix together ¼ cup of milk and 2 well beaten eggs. Salt to taste. (If your owner is going to have some, add a dash of pepper as well.)

Pour back into same pan and scramble until nearly set.

Add crumb mix to pan with eggs.

Cool to warm and share with human. If you're a big dog, double the ingredients.

COMPLETE MACARONI DINNER

Cut up celery and carrots to make up ⅓ cup each.

Add 2 tablespoons of vegetable oil to a hot pan and fry the celery and carrots until they are partially cooked.

Add 12 oz. of either diced meat, meat scraps, or hamburger and cook lightly in the same pan with the vegetables.

Add 2½ cups of water to the frying pan. Mix well and let simmer for 30 minutes.

Cook raw macaroni for 7 minutes in boiling salted water and drain.

Place half the amount of macaroni that you will eat at this meal in your dog dish and top with an equal amount of fried vegetable and meat.

Mix well and serve warm. Freeze leftovers for future use.

GOURMET CANINE COOKIES

Mix 12 oz. enriched white flour with 3 oz. chopped meat scraps.

Add 1 oz. melted fat, roast drippings, or vegetable oil.

Moisten with enough water to give it the consistency you need, and roll out to ¼″ thickness.

Cut into the cookie shape of your choice.

Oil a baking sheet, and bake at 300 °F (150 °C) until crisp.

You can feed the cookies whole or crumble them and mix with other food. Unused cookies can be kept in the refrigerator or frozen for future use.

DIET RECIPE

1 lb cooked ground lean beef
½ lb cooked chopped carrots
½ lb cooked chopped celery
1 chopped hard-boiled egg

Mix all of the ingredients and supplement with vitamins and minerals.

The above recipe is sufficient to feed a 40-pound dog for one day. In order to avoid hunger pains, separate the food into three equal parts and feed one part every 8 hours.

KIDNEY STEW

1 beef kidney
6 tablespoons white flour
1 chopped hard-boiled egg

Wash a fresh kidney and then cut crosswise into ½″ slices and then into small pieces.

Soak in cold water for 15 minutes and drain.

Place in cooking pot, add water, bring to a boil and simmer for 1½ hours without a cover. Let cool.

Mix flour with an equal amount of water and make a paste.

Drain all but 3 cups of liquid from kidney and reheat.

Add flour paste gradually while stirring and cook until thickened. Salt to taste.

Add chopped egg. Mix well.

Serve by mixing with equal amounts of dry dog food or cooked rice.

LAYER CAKE

Cover the bottom of a greased pan with 2 sliced hard-boiled eggs.

Spread 2 oz. chopped raw meat or hamburger over the eggs.

Place more egg slices over the meat.

Add 2 oz. more meat.

Add just enough water to cover and bake at 300 °F (150 °C) for 1 hour.

Mix with an equal volume of dog meal or cooked rice, and serve.

If you think you like mealtime now, just imagine how happy you'll be once your people start fixing tasty goodies like these! You can get them *The Dog Lover's Cookbook* from a local bookstore or by contacting The Main Street Press, William Case House, Pittstown, NJ 08867, (201) 735-9424. ■

Craig Clawborne is the co-author of The 60-Minute Gourmutt.

OKIES
DON INMAN '85

IN AT THE FINISH

Jeremy
227-0187

ccessories make the dog. You can spend hundreds on signer apparel, but the wrong collar or leash will in the look. Distance yourself from the pack with a lection of the best finishing touches, elegant elements to give you that certain je ne sais quoi and guarantee that you're noticed.

BRADLEY OLMAN

0187

MC DUF
CASSIE
CREW

Choices, choices. With so many available colors and patterns to accent his wardrobe, what's a dog to do? Have it all, of course! Opposite page, bandanas for evening wear (rhinestones pick out the subtle detailing of the prints), for work, for sport; each artfully embroidered with your name and number. Match or contrast with champagne safety collars and leads from Gone to the Dogs and offered in flattering hues found nowhere else. Choose fuschia, pewter, burgundy, and ten more pow colors. All at better boutiques or from Petworthies Ltd., 4 Brookside Place, Westport, CT 06880; (203) 227-0187. This page, top, Bandenim bandanas in pure cotton in a rainbow of colors and casual prints for the range rider in you; add your name if you like. At local shops, or from Doggie Denims, Box 1156, Wall, NJ 07719; (201) 280-8444. Bottom, preppy pooches will be drooling over these custom-woven ribbons stitched on high-tensile nylon collars and leads. Each sports solid-brass hardware. At finer department stores and boutiques here and abroad (Harrod's carries its own "H" design). From Up Country, 94 Congdon Street, Providence, RI 02906; (401) 272-8418.

CIRCLE T
CIRCLE T
CIRCLE T
CIRCLE T

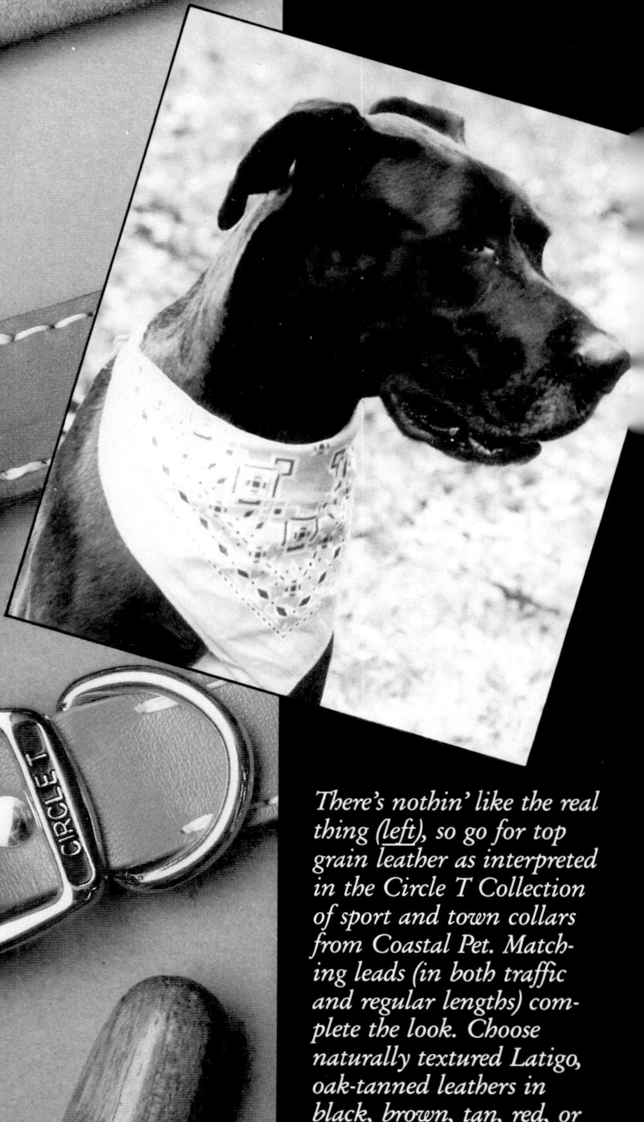

There's nothin' like the real thing (<u>left</u>), so go for top grain leather as interpreted in the Circle T Collection of sport and town collars from Coastal Pet. Matching leads (in both traffic and regular lengths) complete the look. Choose naturally textured Latigo, oak-tanned leathers in black, brown, tan, red, or blue, or for extra richness, order a set in sumptuous suede. At better boutiques or contact Coastal Pet Products, 46 North Rockhill, Alliance, OH 44601; (800) 321-0248. A great look for a Great Dane (<u>inset</u>), this bandana-with-a-difference has cotton batting sewn into its long seam, scented with EPA-approved oil of pennyroyal. The fresh, minty scent is attractive to you and yours, but not to fleas and other unfashionable critters. Of pure cotton in many prints and colors, the Flea-Free bandana comes with a six-month's refresher supply of pennyroyal. At garden and pet shops, or from Woodsman Enterprises, P.O. Box 208, Occoquan, VA 22125; (703) 368-0496.

BRADLEY OLMAN

ollar me handsome: ockwise from top) Top og collars for formal ear in red, white, or blue ith black bow tie, from atherite/Nylorite Mfg., O. Box 145, Carmel, IN 6032. Dapper Dog cor- orate bow tie in proper oard-room silk print from ttle Giant Products, P.O. ox 51, Bogota, NJ 07603. uick-release buckle col- rs in scrumptious colors om Gone to the Dogs, rough Petworthies Ltd., 4 ookside Place, Westport, T 06880; (203) 227-0187. hen only the very best ll do (and of course, u're worth it), a lux- ious alligator collar and sh (with matching belt your owner) and ster- ng silver or silver-plated rdware, by Poochie De- gns exclusively for aren's for People and ts, 1220 Lexington venue, New York, NY 028; (212) 472-9440. do phone home (inset): rsonalized embroidered lon collar in red, blue, ack, orange, or green. ur name and number e in contrasting black or hite. Matching leads and oke collars (also per- nalized) are all exclusive- from Paws 'n Shop, 23 rchwood Circle, Bedford, H 03102; (603) 622-0544.

CASEY

GET-UPS FOR A *GREAT*

Warm, stylish coats create a mood, set the scene, and take you wherever you want to go. Brave the elements in something bold or traditional—it's your choice.

GETAWAY

Plaid rags. . . . ***Opposite page,*** **classic horse-blanket coat makes it easy to travel in style. Made of a practical wool and acrylic blend to alleviate wrinkles** ***en route*****. Traditional tailoring and adjustable buckles for a custom fit. Go wild . . . .** ***This page,*** **water-repellent zebra-stripe raincoat with adjustable buckles and matching leash and collar. Perfect for city streets or the Serengeti. Both coats by Petworthies Ltd., 4 Brookside Place, Westport, CT 06880, (203) 227-0187.**

The call of the wild. . . . Tough, outdoorsy red-and-black lumberjack's coat for camping or hiking trips; soft, warm, and ruggedly handsome, it defies cold weather, wind, and critical observers of your wardrobe. Available from The Dog House, 3 Long Grove Road, Long Grove, IL 60047, (312) 634-3060. If a jaunt through the Appalachians isn't your style, The Dog House can provide you with equally attractive clothes suitable for Aruba, Andalusia, or Anchorage.

CHARLES C. VARGA

BRADLEY OLMAN

To unleash the well-muscled beast within you, we proudly offer Fidoflex. A whole pack of exercises designed to take your body and whippet into shape. All on one simple machine that fits in a corner of your doghouse.

For a free Fidoflex brochure call **1-800-555-FIDO.**

BODY BY FIDOFLEX

FIDOFLEX

Running With Man's Best Friend

A new book offers tips on making it to the top.

Okay, you've decided that you need a little exercise. Your people are complaining that you're lazy, bored, overweight, or disobedient. You also think that you'd like to get some or all of your exercise by running. But regular running is unwise for the uninformed, so here are some precautions:

1. Your breed can make a lot of difference. How good a runner you're likely to be will depend largely on what sort of dog you are. Consult a chart, like the one in Davia Gallup's *Running With Man's Best Friend*, to get a rough idea of your running potential.

2. Start out slowly. Humans don't try to run thirty miles per week immediately. Neither should you.

3. Taking along a human as a running companion can be a lot of fun. Willie, Davia Gallup's Poodle-Terrier cross, started taking her along one day, and they've been jogging together ever since.

4. During warm weather, stop frequently for water. Feel free to lie in puddles, and drink small amounts of water about every twenty minutes. If you notice yourself panting heavily, take a break.

5. If you're running in cold weather and find yourself shivering, try wearing a sweater or a T-shirt on your next run.

6. Always, always, always run on a leash.

7. Make sure you eat a balanced diet—*not* all meat.

8. Running through puddles is apt to get your coat dirty quickly. To make bathing more bearable, rub some mineral oil above your eyes to keep shampoo from getting in, and never use shampoo meant for humans; it's too harsh for a dog's skin.

9. Wear a reflective collar or coat when running after dark.

10. Buy Davia Anne Gallup's *Running With Man's Best Friend* for all of the above tips and more. She'll tell you all about getting started, rest, massage, grooming, diet, and first aid. The book also has a number of photographs, including the ones on these pages, of some very attractive dogs. A must for the canine athlete of any breed. To order, contact: Alpine Publications, Inc., 214 19th Street S.E., Loveland, CO 80537, (303) 667-2017.

JOANNE RUSSELL

SAL A. SESSA

The tall and the short of it: Dachshunds and Danes alike can benefit from a good run. Illustrations from *Running with Man's Best Friend*.

See Spot Run

When Willie, a 20-pound Poodle-Terrier mix, and her person, Davia Gallup, went running, they often saw other dogs and people running together. That gave them an idea. They organized Houston's first annual K-9 Fun Run. It's since become the world's largest race for dogs, and in 1987, with the sponsorship of Ralston-Purina, the Fun Run spread to Atlanta and Los Angeles as well. In a case of seeming anti-canine discrimination, the entry fee per dog is $10, while humans run free, but the event benefits the Humane Society, so it all works out in the end. All contestants receive a dog bowl, a T-shirt, a poster, and a souvenir program. Dogs also get a colorful bandana with which to attach their numbers for the race. In order to compete, you must be leashed and vaccinated for rabies; vets will be on hand in case anyone requires medical attention.

Awards are given in several categories, including large, medium, and small dogs running with male humans and large, medium, and small dogs running with female humans. In addition, contestants are eligible for the following year's Spokesdog contest. To enter write your name, breed, and age on the back of a photograph of yourself at the Fun Run and send it to: Purina Hi Pro K-9 Fun Run, 2303 Sunset Boulevard, Houston, TX. For more information on the Fun Run or the Spokesdog contest, call (713) 521-9187.

K9 FUN RUN

DALE O'DELL

Sonny, the 1987 Fun Run Spokesdog, is a two-year-old Shepherd/Labrador mix who enjoys tennis and softball as well as running, but you don't need to be the best of athletes to be a Spokesdog. "The primary qualities you need," says Sonny, "are friendliness and enthusiasm."

The Houston Fun Run gets underway.

Suit Yourself

Biting winds and nippy mornings can discourage the most dedicated of runners. Fight back with gear designed for chilly Chows and shivering Shelties. T-shirts from Dee Pet Products are perfect for early morning runs, and a rugged gray jogging suit from Ben Richter will get Old Dog Winter off your heels. The suit is available in sizes 10 to 30. For information on the T-shirts, contact: Dee Pet Products, P.O. Box 199, Argyle, TX 76226, (817) 464-7706. Ben Richter Designs are available through better pet stores.

BRADLEY OLMAN

BRADLEY OLMAN

Ruff and Tuff

The Kong Company's Tuffy products are built for dogs who give their toys a fierce workout. **Tuffy** toys will be replaced with no questions asked by the company's president, Joe Markham, if you don't like them or are able to destroy them. Three sizes are available: large, for dogs thirty pounds or over; medium, for those weighing ten to twenty-nine pounds; and small, for dogs under ten pounds. The unique shape, unpredictable bouncing pattern, and hard rubber construction of Tuffy toys offer several advantages: Tuffy cleans teeth, stimulates gums, strengthens jaw muscles, relieves tension, sharpens reflexes, acts as a substitute for things too valuable or dangerous to chew, won't mark walls or floors, and can be washed in the dishwasher. To order, contact: The Kong Co., 300 S. Lamar Court, Lakewood, CO 80226, (303) 934-9958.

Gonna Fly Now

You know you've seen them. They're in the parks, on the beaches, and maybe even on your street. They always look as if they're having more fun than the other dogs. Their people look proud of them and brag about them to the other humans. And it's all because they can jump into the air and catch a frisbee.

Don't let your lack of skill worry you. Even the most accomplished frisbee-catchers had to start somewhere, and **Flying Dog** will help you get off the ground. It's a cassette and special flying disk that will teach your human to throw a frisbee properly and teach you to catch one. The special disk even has a place for a dog biscuit, so you can reward yourself immediately for a successful catch. For more information, call or write: BKW Pet Research, 18 Azalea Lane, San Carlos, CA 94070, (415) 595-3195.

Flying Dog
FLYING DOG™ PROVEN TRAINING SYSTEM
Tested and Proven with Big and Small Dogs Like Yours!
Flying Dog
BKW Pet Research

Have A Ball

One of the best ways to get in shape is to work out with weights, and even if you can't lift them, you can get a lot of exercise from rolling them. Yes, you read this right—*rolling them*. The Boomer Ball and the Canine Castle Exercise Ball are weighted balls designed to be rolled and chased rather than thrown or chewed. In fact, the **Boomer Ball** comes with a one-year guarantee: if you can bite or chew a hole in it, the company will replace it free of charge. The balls can't injure you, although you should only play with them in an enclosed area, because in your concentration on the game, you may lose track of what's going on around you. The durable, plastic Boomer Ball has a ⅛″-thick sidewall and comes in red, yellow, orange, and blue. Three sizes are available. The largest is 10″ in diameter, weighs two pounds, and costs $17. It has an access plug, so you can add pebbles to create a rattling noise as you play or water or sand to make the ball heavier for a tougher workout. The 6″ and 4½″ Boomer Balls, which do not have access plugs, cost $12 each and weigh ¼ pound and ⅛ pound, respectively. The company will soon be releasing a new product, **BoomeRound**, a 6″, off-balance, weighted ball which will roll erratically and rock as it stops. It's all one piece, has no moving parts, and will cost $15. To order, contact: Boomer Ball, P.O. Box 83, Grayslake, IL 60030, (312) 546-6125.

D.J. PHOTOGRAPHY

Boomer, the namesake of the Boomer Ball and Spuds MacKenzie's litter sister, demonstrates workout techniques.

The **Canine Castle Exercise Ball** is similar to the Boomer Ball. It is slightly heavier; the 10″ ball weighs 2½ pounds, and the 8″ ball weighs 1½ pounds. Both balls have access plugs and are available in blue, green, and brown. Get your friends together and start a bassetball team! To order, call or write: Canine Castle, P.O. Box 1059, Brownwood, TX 76801, (915) 643-2517. Outside Texas, call toll-free: (800) 351-1363.

Canine Castle offers two exercise balls designed to give you a husky build.

MUSH! Panting for the Gold

BY BERNARD MALAMUTE

Gee! Haw! Straight ahead! The commands ring out in the crystalline air. And the superbly conditioned Huskies respond effortlessly to the words of their drivers in the race to be first and best. Neither bitter cold, arctic winds, nor blinding snows deter these brave champions—they think only of that ultimate finish line.

Hundreds of years of breeding have gone into the making of these virile modern athletes whose competitors are a frozen landscape, unpredictable weather conditions, and each other. But while today's Huskies run for the sport of it, their forefathers ran for their very survival. Early sled dogs were critical to the lives of the Eskimos and Indians who were once the only inhabitants of the frozen northlands. Used for transportation, for protection, for hunting and trapping, and for companionship, the dogs were indispensable family members. Their bravery and endurance are the stuff of legend. In the 1870s, the Royal Canadian Mounted Police used sled teams to help bring order to the northern frontier. Later, sled dogs enabled explorers such as Byrd, Peary, and Amundsen to traverse the polar ice caps. Yet one of the most incredible feats those early heroes performed is little remembered today. In the winter of 1925, nearly two dozen native and U.S. Mail sled dog teams were hastily organized to rush life-saving toxin from Anchorage to Nome, a distance of more than a thousand miles, to help combat an outbreak of dreaded diptheria.

Their modern counterparts, no less athletic, show the same spirit and drive as they race for the gold. To see the best of them in action, follow the calendar of the International Sled Dog Racing Association, governing body of the sport, which sanctions more than 150 races each year with total prize money in excess of half a million dollars. The largest and most prestigious of these events, the ALPO International Sled Dog Races, is held each January in Saranac Lake, New York. With prize money of $50,000, it is the sport's single biggest payday. Competitions

ALPO PETFOODS, INC.

ALPO
ALPO
28

SLED
DOGS
IONAL

ALPO PETFOODS, INC.

are held in various classifications, including three-dog, six-dog, eight-dog, and unlimited. Plan to attend to howl for your team.

For information about specific races, contact the International Sled Dog Racing Association (ISDRA), c/o Donna Hawley, P.O. Box 446, Norman, ID 83848-0446, or ALPO Petfoods, Inc., P.O. Box 2187, Allentown, PA 18001, (215) 398-4646. ■

. . . .

Bernard Malamute's latest books include The Foxhound, Dachshund's Lives, *and* The Magic Basset.

The competition is keen (*opposite page*) as two of the nearly two hundred dog teams entered in Alpo's 9th annual race head for the finish line in Lake Placid, New York. In a quieter moment (*above*), one of the athletes takes time out to make a new friend, while another (*below*), contemplates races won and races to come.

ALPO PETFOODS, INC

And the winner is....

IDITAROD CHAMPIONS
'87
PRO PLAN
Purina PRO PLAN
IDITAROD TRAIL
ALASKA

RALSTON PURINA COMPANY

Current champions of Alaska's grueling Iditarod Trail Race, a 1,100-mile odyssey from Anchorage to Nome that crosses some of the most unforgiving country in the world, are Granite and one of his teammates, Sluggo (foreground), shown celebrating their most recent victory with musher / owner Susan Butcher. Granite is at the top of dogdom in Alaska, having led the Purina-sponsored Butcher / Pro Plan Sled Dog Team to two consecutive record-breaking Iditarod triumphs. Like other Alaskan Huskies from Butcher's renowned Trailbreaker Kennels, Granite is as tough as his name suggests. And like his owner, he is singled-minded; his acute sense of smell keeps him hot on the scent of victory.

Interiors

CREATURE COMFORTS
by I.M. Shar-pei

The bed or doghouse you select says much about you. It represents the essence of your private life and is as personal and as individual as a pawprint. Yet, like a pawprint, it invites interpretation. Those who know you will see in your living space a reflection of your self-perception. So think carefully before you go house-hunting or bed-buying. What image do you want to project, and how do you think of yourself? As rugged? Pampered? Practical? Stylish?

Whether your primary consideration is aesthetic appeal, attention to detail, comfort,

Elegant manorisms. . . . Animal Manors brings dreams to life with designer homes built to any size specifications. For indoor or outdoor use, these homes are distinguished by their crucial attention to detail, superb architectural mastery, and a range of styles limited only by your imagination. Continental flavor. . . .*This page*, the French Chateau Elaborée, with traditional mansard roof (which removes for easy cleaning), and high, formal windows. Walls may be tapestried or finished in salon red, and the center shield may bear your coat of arms. Marble floors keep you cool in summer and are covered with a down-filled, cedar-lined brocade cushion in winter. The perfect spot. . . .*Opposite page, top*, the Mod Dog Pad, the ultimate residence for the lone wolf. Racy details like a 1930s hood ornament above the door, a zebra-striped cushion, and a liberal use of Plexiglass and Pirelli rubber create a feeling of action and excitement. Chrome-and-black color scheme completes the effect. Small-town charm. . . .*Bottom*, an all-wood New England cottage, designed for quiet relaxation. Its pairs of windows and tall chimney evoke images of simplicity and tranquility. For more information about Animal Manors, contact the company at: 462 W. 23rd St., Suite 1, New York, NY 10011, (212) 206-6231.

DAN BARBA

Interiors

practicality, or affordability, there's a bed or doghouse built to suit your particular needs. Sizes, colors, styles, prices, and special features are almost unlimited. All you need to know is where to look, and on the next pages we'll show you where—and give you a glimpse of some of the most noteworthy products on the market, from brass beds to waterbeds and from pup tents to marble-floored chateaux. Indoors or outdoors, you'll finally have the image you've always wanted—and the perfect bed or house you've always needed. ■

The windows of I.M. Shar-pei's Hancocker Building can be found throughout Boston.

Outdoorsy dogs will feel right at home in this tent from Digger Specialties. Portable, durable, rust-proof, and mosquito-netted, it comes in red, blue, green, and brown. Three sizes are available: small, which is 16″ wide and 20″ long and costs $69.95; medium, which is 24″ by 30″ and costs $94.95; and large, which is 37″ by 45″ and costs $129.95. All prices include shipping and handling. Write: Digger Specialties, P.O. Box 42, Bremen, IN 46506.

To look and feel relaxed, you need a supremely comfortable bed, like the Small Waves waterbed, *above*. The fire-, stain-, and tear-resistant vinyl cover is easily cleaned, reduces odors, and won't soak through, rot, or mildew. Permanent antibacterial and antifungal treatments enhance your comfort. The three sizes range in price from $49.95 to $79.95 and in dimensions from 20″ by 24″ to 32″ by 44″. For more information, contact: Small Waves, 1145-H Dominguez, Carson, CA 90746, (213) 604-0504. *Below*, comfort takes on a classic look. This polyester-and-cedar-filled cushion has a removable, washable cover and comes in tan, brown, red plaid, and blue plaid. Sizes range from 24″ to 42″ in diameter. Contact: Pedigrees, 15 Turner Drive, Spencerport, NY 14559, (716) 352-1232.

An electric bed beats electric blankets paws down, *top.* Special features include variable heat settings, the absence of moving parts, and a cord designed to discourage chewing. Best of all, it won't cut your income to the bone, since it uses no more power than a 60-watt bulb. Sizes range from 12½" by 18½" to 22½" by 28½". Contact: Lectro-Kennel, P.O. Box 9281, 310 Tia Juana, Colorado Springs, CO 80932, (303) 633-0404. *Center*, the warm acrylic cover and soft walls of the Fur Cuddler are designed for comfort, but convenience hasn't been overlooked. Assorted colors let you match your home's decor, and five sizes, ranging from 21" to 43" in diameter, fit almost any breed. Contact: Flexi-Mat, 2244 S. Western Ave., Chicago, IL 60608, (312) 376-5500. *Bottom,* the Canine Castle Pup Hut is the practical dog's dream house. The non-porous surface keeps fleas from breeding in it, and adjustable fasteners let you raise the roof slightly for 360° ventilation in the summer. A center floor drain makes cleaning easy, and the overhanging roof keeps it watertight. To keep it cool, the Pup Hut's roof is white, but you may choose gold, red, green, navy, or brown for the bottom. It measures 30½" long, 25" wide, and 20" high and carries a five-year limited warranty. Contact: Canine Castle, P.O. Box 1059, Brownwood, TX 76801, (800) 351-1363. In Texas, call: (915) 643-2517.

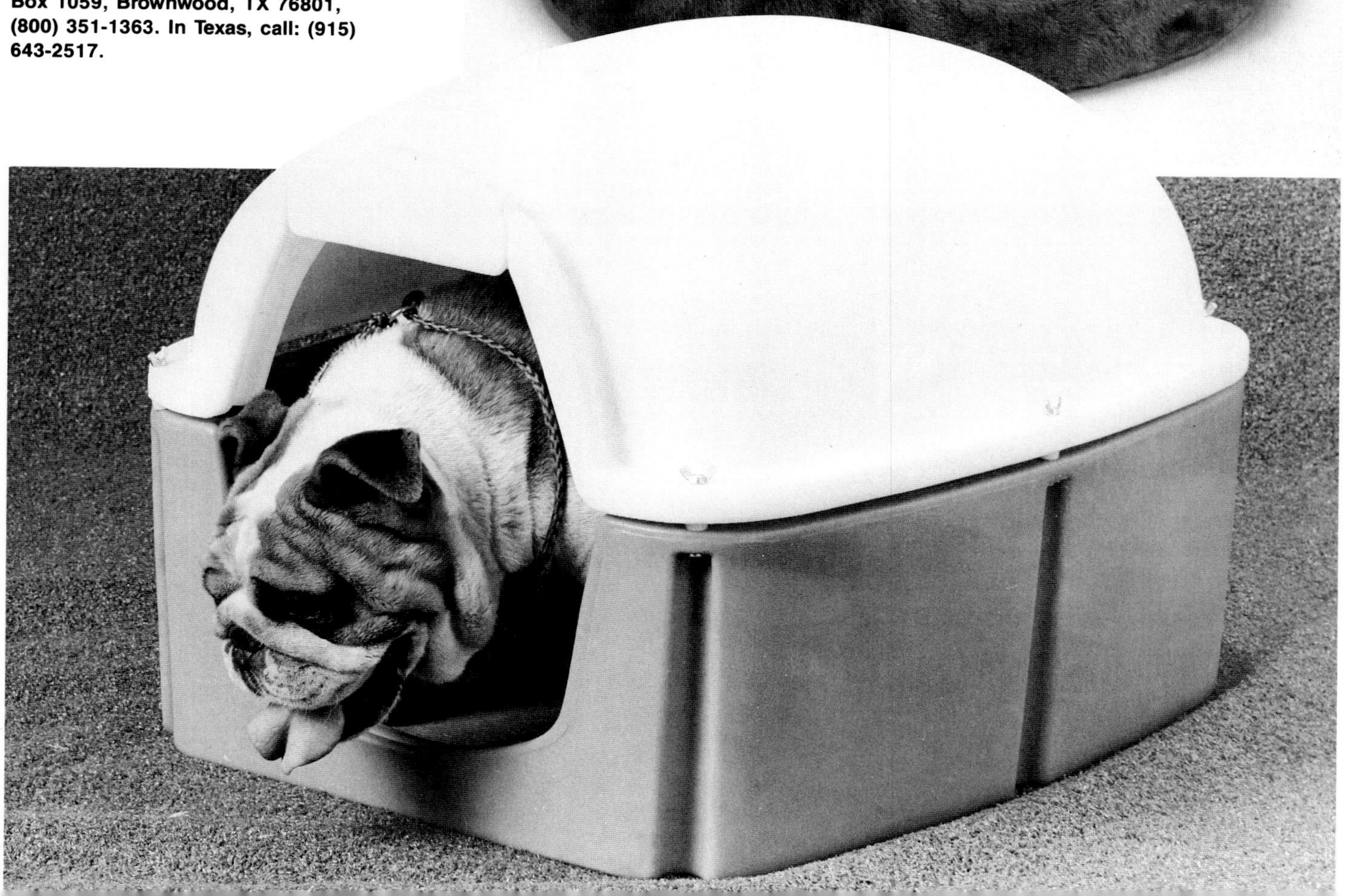

Interiors

BRADLEY OLMAN

The top of the line, fo the dog who wants hi bed to reflect his own elegance, sophistication, and confidence. *Bottom left* and *top*, Animal Manors' collec tion of beds and baskets, designed by Cynthia Cobey. Match ing quilts and futons can be rolled and tie for portability, and cedar-filled matching fabric bones act as a attractive, natural, an aromatic pest repelle Basket cushions may filled with cedar, dow or a variety of machi washable materials, a the covers are availab in designer fabrics. *Bottom right*, a chais designed by Jamie Hanson, that says you've got it all. A fa travertine platform derives an air of cultured solidity from eight large gold spheres. The cushion down-filled and has a thin, cedar-filled inne cushion on the botto Covered with turquoi velvet edged with gol lamé piping, it's a resting place like no other, and can be bui to any size specifications. For more inform tion on Animal Mano designer beds, conta the company at: 462 West 23rd Street, Ne York, NY 10011, (212) 206-6231.

DAN BARBA

Get Up and Go—In Safety and Comfort

by Greyhound Greene

It's time to escape. Time to get a change of scenery. To go where uniformed attendants pamper you, or simply to someplace far away from civilization as you know it.

But you'd be mad simply to dart from your doghouse and race in any direction. Travel requires planning, and the first step is to choose your destination. What pekes [sic] your interest? What gives you a case of wanderlust that itches more than the worst case of fleas? The cold, wild waters of the Chesapeake Bay? The hot sun of Chihuahua? The Yorkshire moors?

Once you know where you're headed, think about how you'd like to travel. If you're planning on flying, it's best to travel with your people, since it's generally less expensive and more comfortable to do so. If, however, you have to travel alone for some reason, don't plan the trip alone. Call **Air Animal**.

Established by veterinarian Walter M. Woolf and his wife Millie in 1977, Air Animal will arrange everything for you. The company will provide transportation to the airport in an air-conditioned van, any necessary ground services including grooming and veterinary care, CAB- and USDA-approved flight kennels with your name and the name of the human you're meeting attached, health insurance, and temporary boarding if necessary. The Woolfs will get you on the right plane, give your people the flight number and air waybill, and tell them where and when to pick you up. They move about twenty animals each week in the United States and overseas, and their minimum charge is $60. For information, contact: Air Animal Inc., 4120 West Cypress St., Tampa, FL 33607-2358, (813) 879-3210.

TIPS FOR AIRLINE TRAVEL

1. Call ahead before you leave for the airport. Regulations prohibit dogs from traveling by air when the temperature is above or below a certain point. Always check on the day of your trip to make sure you'll be allowed to get on the plane.

2. Don't eat on the day of the flight. It's also a good idea not to drink for 4 to 6 hours beforehand.

3. Don't submit to sedation. There's no need for it, and it may be dangerous.

4. Don't wear a collar or harness while flying.

5. Don't take any toys, bones, etc. with you in the flight kennel.

6. Try out the kennel before the day of the flight. You'll be a lot less nervous if you're used to it.

7. For twenty-four hours after the flight, take food and water in small amounts only.

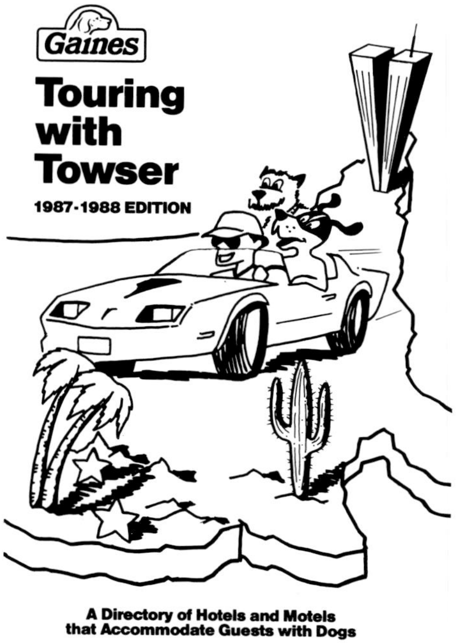
Gaines
Touring with Towser
1987-1988 EDITION
A Directory of Hotels and Motels that Accommodate Guests with Dogs

If you're going cross-country by car with your people, you'll need to find places to stop for the night. And, sadly, some of the most luxurious and scenic hotels in the United States refuse to give reservations to dogs, no matter how charming, intelligent, or sophisticated they may be. To save gas, time, and the embarrassment of a rejection, use a guide to hotels and motels that will greet you with open paws. Gaines's ***Touring with Towser***, first published in 1948, is an excellent example. The current edition contains listings for over 2500 independently owned establishments and nine nationwide chains with over 4500 locations. Addresses and telephone numbers are included, so you can make reservations by mail or phone, as you prefer. The 80-page book contains coupons for Gaines and Ken-L Ration products. To order, send a check for $1.50 to: Gaines *Touring with Towser*, P.O. Box 5700, Kankakee, IL 60902. Dog clubs wishing to buy the guides in quantity at a discount for fund-raising should request a quantity order form from: Gaines Dog Care Center, P.O. Box 9001, Chicago, IL 60604-9001.

Of course, it's possible that you'd rather not stay in a hotel for people. Such establishments, however pleased they may be to welcome you, generally cater more to the humans in your party. If you're looking for a little V.I.P. treatment, like grooming or bathing services or a special exercise area for dogs, forget it. Pet hotels, on the other hand, are especially designed to meet your needs.

If you're planning to stay in California, the **Holiday Pet Hotel**, located in Encinitas, may meet with your approval. The kennels, which can be interconnected if you're traveling *a deux*, feature sturdy wire set in carefully crafted oak frames, indoor/outdoor runs, state-of-the-art convection heating and cooling, and space for sixty dogs. Attendants are on the premises twenty-four hours a day, and an intercom system constantly monitors all parts of the kennels, so you need only bark and service is at hand. The intercoms serve another function as well, sending soothing music to your pen to calm you and lend elegance to your meals. Jenny Perkins, the owner of the Holiday Pet Hotel, prides herself on its cleanliness, friendliness, and attentiveness to guests. Cats have a separate wing, so you can keep your distance easily. There's nothing like a scratched nose to spoil a vacation.

Everything at the Holiday Pet Hotel is regulated for the comfort and convenience of its guests. Exercise areas are spacious; exterior runs have concrete block dividers 20″ to 40″ high beneath the normal fencing to assure you of maximum privacy. You'll receive daily handling and be called by name, and, if you're ill, your own vet will be notified first if possible. If he or she is unavailable, the closest available vet will be consulted. Your people, of course, will be required to pay the bills. Feel free to bring any toys you like; you may also bring your own food or sample Holiday's high-quality, nutritionally balanced diet at no extra cost.

Make sure you're clean and parasite-free before you check in; if external parasites, skin conditions, or particularly long nails are

JOE COYLE

Kiska enjoys the deluxe accommodations at the Holiday Pet Hotel.

Knowing your options is the key to a great vacation.

JOE COYLE

HOLIDAY PET HOTEL
HOLIDAY PE
753-6754

Leave the driving to them . . . ride to your vacation retreat in style in Holiday Pet Hotel's chauffeured transportation. A comfortable, raised bed awaits you, so you can relax as soon as you arrive.

discovered, Holiday will treat you for the problems to insure the comfort of all guests—at your people's expense. The kennel has no inside grooming service, but cleansing, medicated baths, hot oil treatments, and coat conditioning are available. Regular clients on extended visits may also arrange for a trim. Remember that baths may be necessary during a hotel stay for puppies, dogs with long hair, or older dogs; however, Holiday offers complimentary baths to short-coated dogs and half-price baths to all dogs staying five nights or more.

Daily rates are quite reasonable and are contingent upon your size. Small dogs are $9 per night, medium dogs $10, large dogs $11, and giant dogs $13. Special services can also be obtained for nominal fees. Arrangements to exercise without an attendant in a large play yard can be made for $2 per day. The same $2 fee also allows a kennel mate to join you if you like. V.I.P. treatment, which costs $4 per day for one dog and $6 per day for two dogs together, includes play time and individualized attention; an attendant will play ball with you, brush you daily, give you special treats, read postcards from your people, play cassettes of their voices, or whatever else you specify. For only $3 per day, you may reside in the Special Care Ward—this fee and the accompanying advantages may be made mandatory at Holiday's discretion. This ward is ideal for older, shy, disabled, convalescent, or very young dogs. It features rugs, a rocking chair, sunny patio areas, an especially quiet exercise area, and attentive caretakers who'll provide you with a special diet or with medication if necessary.

Holiday's office hours are: Monday-Friday, 9:00-5:00; Saturday, 9:00-noon; and Sunday, 2-4. Check-out time is noon; if you leave before that time, you will not be charged for that night's lodging. The kennel is closed on major holidays and occasionally the day before or the day after. For more information, contact: Holiday Pet Hotel, 551 Union St., Encinitas, CA 92024, (619) 753-6754.

Those seeking a counterpart to Holiday's services in the Midwest might want to try the **American Pet Motel**. Standard amenities include twice-daily feedings for puppies and Great Danes, off-floor beds, a balanced diet and bedtime "cookie" break or the freedom to bring your favorite food, reading of letters and cards from your people at no charge, playing of cassettes of your people's voices at no charge, air conditioning, heating, soft music twenty-four hours a day, and constant-fill water bowls. Tranquilizers are never used to quiet noisy dogs, and there are no cages. Instead, you check into a room with free access to and from an outside patio.

The American Pet Motel is designed and built for dogs. Special exhaust systems change the air in your room twenty times each hour, and air is never mixed between kennels, so you're at less risk from airborne disease. Even the grooming parlor has its own air system. The company has such confidence in this system that it offers you, for only $2.05, health insurance that covers you for illness, injury, or death for any reason while you're boarding. Your room and patio are sanitized daily for extra safety.

Special services are also available at the American Pet Motel. Bathing and nail trimming range in cost from $9 for a Basenji to $25 for a Komondor, Old English Sheepdog, St. Bernard, Great Pyrenees, or Newfoundland. Medicated baths cost $5 extra. If you want to go for the works, American also offers grooming services, hot oil treatments, flea and tick baths and dips, towels for your bed, on-leash exercise, and door-to-door limousine service. Veterinary attention can be arranged during your stay for the cost of the vet's bill plus a $2 fee.

American offers three types of accommodations to suit any income and lifestyle. Deluxe rooms come with plastic off-floor beds, partial carpeting, and the bedtime cookie break. Each kennel has no more than 50 rooms and has a full-time attendant and night lights. Imperial accommodations have fewer dogs per kennel, meaning that you get more attention from your attendant and less noise from other dogs. The

TIPS FOR HOTEL STAYS

1. Always check the boarding area before checking in. If the kennel won't show you where you'll be staying before they get their money, be suspicious.

2. Make sure you've had all the necessary vaccinations before checking in, and ask the kennel which ones they require. Holiday Pet Hotel, for example, asks for proof that you've had vaccinations for DHLP & P, Rabies, and Bordetella, while Sky Run only requires DHLP & P.

3. After you complete your stay and return home, be careful not to overeat, overdrink, or overplay. Too much food, water, or excitement right away could make you feel unwell.

The American Pet Motel.

American Pet Motel welcomes a guest.

rooms themselves have full carpeting and brass beds with foam-rubber mattresses. Attendants will brush you daily, spend time playing with you, and give you an extra cookie break. Regency Suites measure 6′ by 6′ and include all the features of Imperial rooms plus daily on-leash exercise. Prices per night depend on your size, the size of your room, whether or not you choose to share it with a friend, and what type of service you prefer. They range from $7 a night for a small dog in a small Deluxe room to $20 a night for a Great Dane in a Regency Suite.

Bedtime or bone time in a Regency suite at the American Pet Motel.

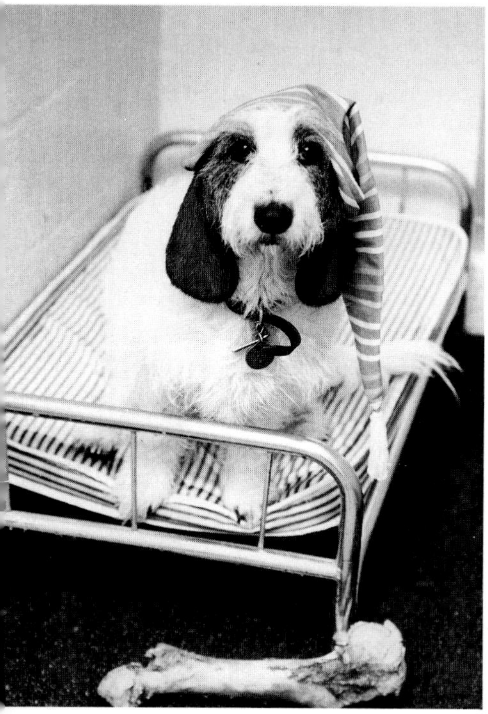

American's office hours are: Monday and Friday, 9-1 and 2-7; Tuesday, Thursday and Saturday, 9-1 and 2-5; and Wednesday, Sunday, and holidays, closed. You may check in at any time, but you must check out by 1:00. The kennel also offers an air travel service in conjunction with American Airlines. Together, the companies can offer airline reservations and tickets, door-to-door delivery in most major cities around the world, temporary kenneling if desired, rental and sale of four sizes of government-approved travel kennels, twenty-four-hour veterinary coverage, and arrangements for health certificates, travel documents, public health and customs clearances, quarantine arrangements for foreign travel, and foreign consulate clearances. For more information, contact: American Pet Motels, Inc., 22096 North Pet Lane, Prairie View, IL 60069, (312) 634-9444.

If a quiet vacation in a mountain retreat appeals to you, consider Barbara Skinner's **Sky Run Kennel**. Skinner raises AKC Borzois, AKC Collies, and Border Collies, so she knows what dogs like. She'll cater to your comfort on her twenty-two acres, offering you large, comfortable accommodations, plenty of exercise, home cooking, and safety. Her indoor/outdoor runs measure 16′ to 50′ and give you complete freedom of access to keep you active, safe, secure, clean, and comfortable. The fare consists of top-quality feed, ground beef, and venison. Breakfast, a special diet, or medication can be incorporated into the kennel's routine on request.

Veterinary care is only two miles away and on call twenty-four hours a day. The runs feature hot water heat at dog level and plenty of rugs and blankets in winter; the building is air cooled in summer, while outside, cool mountain breezes and tall, shady pines beckon. A five-acre fenced exercise field keeps you in perfect shape. Bring your own toys or swim in the spring-fed "cement pond." You'll also receive weekly baths and daily brushing.

While you're at Sky Run, take the opportunity to pick up some social graces. Skinner offers obedience courses designed to improve your manners and your air of sophistication. Your people can learn something, too; lessons in show handling will teach them how to prove that you're a top dog. For reservations or a tour of the facilities, contact: Sky Run Kennel, R.D. 1, Box 36, Stewartsville, NJ 08886, (201) 859-4554.

Wherever you go, travel safely and find a place to stay where people care about your comfort. After all, you don't want to miss any of the sunshine, the snow, the waves, the woods, or the sweet relaxation. ■

Greyhound Greene's books include The Tenth Dog, The Canine Factor, *and* The Confidential Afghan.

PET PASSPORT™

It's bad enough being left behind when your owners take a vacation, but it's even worse when you're left with someone who knows nothing about you. You can make things a little easier with a Pet Passport from Innovative Amenities. It has everything a temporary caretaker needs to know: the names of your people, your vital statistics, your photograph and noseprint, dietary guidelines, personality profile, notes on veterinary care, medical record, family history, and show records. There are also travel tips, a travel diary, and places for the stamps of states and countries. The Pet Passport is not an official document, but Presidential dogs Rex and Lucky have them, so how much more official could you get? For more information, contact: Innovative Amenities, 1021 Lincoln Blvd., Suite 217, Santa Monica, CA 90403, (213) 394-6992.

ART

Canines Captured On Canvas

ROGER APPLEBY

***Above,* Norton's striking portrait of Mrs. William F. Buckley, Jr., and her dogs. *Left,* a detail of a King Charles Cavalier Spaniel demonstrates Norton's skill with a brush.**

ROGER APPLEBY

Whether your taste runs to nineteenth-century hunting scenes or portraits of yourself and your human companions, there's nothing like a work of art to give your home a touch of sheer elegance. Fine paintings can turn a kennel into a castle and a doghouse into a dream house. We'd like to call your attention to two sources of dignified artwork that lend a well-bred atmosphere to your surroundings.

Seekers of eternal fame, those wishing to found a dognasty, or those who simply have a touch of well-deserved pride may wish to contact British artist John Norton. Norton requests that your owners sit with you, as he does not paint portraits of individual dogs. He notes our understandable nervousness at being recorded for posterity and our resulting restless behavior, but, unlike many painters, he doesn't exclude us from the family portrait on those grounds. He enjoys including both dogs and humans in his paintings, believing that a domestic scene gains much from the representation of both.

Norton specializes in capturing a dog's personality. He pays careful attention to a dog's movements and behavior, not only when he's painting, but from the moment he and his model are introduced. The results are portraits that capture the distinctive characteristics of both the breed and the individual. If you would like to commission Norton to paint you and your owners, contact his United States representative, Leigh Westbrook, at: Petsmarts Inc., 225 West 35th Street, New York, NY 10001, (212) 947-5740 or 947-5755.

If you prefer a painting with a little history, you might wish to contact Schillay & Rehs. This gallery features fine oil paintings, many of which portray dogs in domestic or sporting scenes. Among such works are paintings by George Armfield (c. 1808-1893), who spent his life meeting the growing demand for portraits of domestic animals and who specialized in paintings of terriers or spaniels hunting; by Gustave Leonard de Jonghe, son of the landscape artist Jean-Baptiste de Jonghe; and by Charles Burton Barber, who painted portraits of Queen Victoria's dogs and grandchildren from the early 1870's until his death in 1894.

To find out more about the fine paintings offered by Schillay & Rehs, contact: Schillay & Rehs, Inc., 305 E. 63rd Street, New York, NY 10021, (212) 355-5710. The gallery is open Monday to Friday, 9:30-5:00, and on Saturdays by appointment.

Samples of nineteenth-century paintings handled by Schillay & Rehs. *Top left*, "Terriers Rabbiting" by George Armfield. *Top right,* "Afternoon Repose" by Gustave Leonard de Jonghe. *Bottom,* "Off to School" by Charles Burton Barber.

If you're partial to a little nip in your doggie dish, drop us a line. We like sniffing out new friends.

AT JACK SPANIEL'S DISTILLERY, litters upon litters of puppies have grown up making our fine whiskey as their fathers did. Working in this sturdy, picturesque building, they learn the tricks of the trade early, carrying on a family tradition.

We take traditions seriously at Jack Spaniel's. Ours have lasted 121 years (that's 847 in dog years). We think that once you take a sip of our whiskey, you'll be glad we know how to teach a new dog old tricks.

JACK SPANIEL'S
OLD TIME
QUALITY
Tennessee
SOUR MASH
WHISKEY
BOTTLED AT THE DISTILLERY

SMOOTH LICKIN' TENNESSEE WHISKEY

Tennessee Whiskey • 81-91 Proof • Distilled and Bottled by Jack Spaniel's Distillery
Clem Muttlow, Proprietor, Route 2, Tickburg, Tennessee.

She knew that she was just another bitch to him, but it didn't matter.

TO ONE I LOVE

The Other Side of Milkbone

By Sidney Sheltie

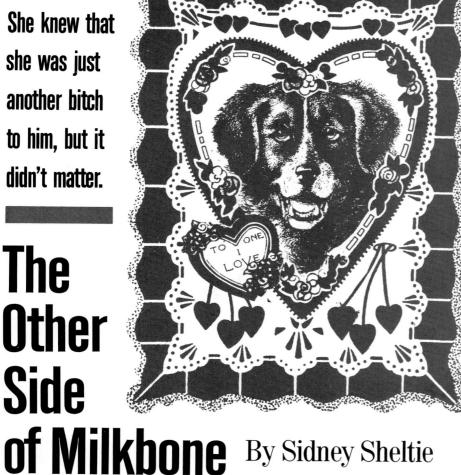

Noelle Pug sat on the couch near the window sill, gazing through the gleaming panes into the deep purple night beyond. The air, she knew, would be cool and fresh, and she waited anxiously for the call she knew would come.

A human entered the room. He was tall, very tall, with graying hair and kind eyes. Noelle hated to hurt him, but it was not a matter of choice. She felt compelled to do what she had planned, compelled by a force she hardly understood.

"Time to go outside, Noelle," he said softly. There seemed to be a trace of sadness in his voice. *Could he know? Could he have found out somehow? No. Never. Humans weren't that intelligent.* She glanced from the window to him, scrutinizing his face. *No, he knew nothing.* She drew her lips slowly from her teeth in a smirk.

"What a beautiful smile," he cooed appreciatively. "Come on, now."

She leapt from the couch and followed him.

They had arranged everything last night, the two of them, while they crouched near the azaleas in the back yard.

He had appeared earlier, seemingly from the darkness itself, and she had frozen, half frightened, half attracted by the strange scent floating toward her.

"Who's there?" she yelped.

"My name's Larry," returned a reassuring bark. "Larry Doglas." He stepped into the yard and let the moonlight shine on his fur.

"I'm Noelle," she said. She walked toward him, drawn to him against her will by an animal magnetism that she found irresistible. She knew that she was just another bitch to him, that she would never see him again, but it didn't matter.

Afterward, after cigarettes, she had expected him to leave immediately, to run back to his own yard, wherever that was. But he stayed.

"You're so beautiful," he whimpered. "Your coat is so sleek, so smooth. The curl in your tail drives me wild. And that darling moist nose that turns heavenward while remaining passionately earthbound!"

"Oh Larry, I love you."

He started a little and stared at her. She met his gaze for a few seconds and then looked away.

"Let's run away together," he barked excitedly. "Tomorrow night. When you go for your walk, I'll meet you, and we'll leave together."

"Do you mean it?" Her tail began to wag.

"Of course I mean it." He gave her a lick or two. "I have to go now, but I'll be back tomorrow night. I promise."

Noelle had waited all day, panting with anticipation. She knew that what she was doing was wrong, was foolish, but she didn't care. Doglas brought out the animal in her, and if he told her to heel, she knew she must obey.

Her human's touch was suddenly repulsive to her. It was so calm, so dispassionate. She became aware, as she had never been before, that she was just a dog to him. He thought of her as a *pet.* And she had allowed herself to think of him as an equal, a friend. She had been fooling herself.

She thought of Larry's words, *I'll be back tomorrow night, I promise,* and none of it mattered. All that mattered now was Larry Doglas. She would give herself to him completely, and everything would be all right.

She stepped into the cool night and watched the door to the house close. In five minutes the human would call for her again. She sniffed the air for traces of Larry.

He was not there.

Maybe he was wounded in a dogfight. Maybe he couldn't get out of his house. She thought of a dozen reasons for his absence, believing none of them. She knew the truth.

He had lied to her. He was just like all the others, a dirty, lying dog, and he didn't deserve to live. She stood in her yard, trembling with rage. She could not go back into that house. Nothing would be the same. Noelle began to walk away in the darkness. She would never go back, never. And she would have her revenge one day. She would dog Larry's steps, and one day he would make a mistake. Meanwhile, a world of power, designer chew toys, and gourmet dog food awaited, if she could reach out and seize it. Her day would come. ■

(To be continued)

Sidney Sheltie's other novels include Master of the Dane *and* Rage of Airedales.

The Hounda engineers are full of surprises these days. You'd think after our previous successes, we'd be resting on our laurels.

Instead, we're introducing a racy little bag of tricks called the CRM. It stands for Canine Road Machine, and it's sheer magic.

For its first trick, the Hounda CRM will go from zero to sixty in 7.9 seconds. Then we'll have it impress you with its roomy interior, smooth ride, sleek exterior, and surprisingly low price. If you're really in a de-

manding mood, we'll even have it jump through a ring of fire.

In fact, we can only think of one trick that the CRM can't do. Play dead.

Test drive a new Hounda CRM today and discover why other engineers think of us as magicians. Or you could wait until we outdo ourselves again.

For our next trick we'll make the competition roll over.

For economy, styling, reliability, and handling, there's nothing like a

HOUNDA

Off the Collar

NEED A LIFT?

A small dog doesn't have to go to the jungle, the ocean, or the desert to find adventure; there's plenty of it on every city street. Fierce Dobermans, busy streets, elevators, revolving doors, and packs of people can overwhelm the stoutest of heart and sharpest of tooth. To stay serene while chaos reigns about you, get a **Doggie Bag.** It's comfortable, with adjustable Velcro straps, plenty of firm chest support, and three sizes: small, for dogs under eight pounds; medium, for dogs weighing eight to twelve pounds; and large, for twelve to eighteen-pound dogs. Your people won't strain your back by picking you up clumsily, and you won't get muddy paws on their clothes. It's easy to put on and take off, and it comes in a wide array of bold, fashionable colors, including red, black, blue, and Scottish plaid. It even doubles as a harness for walking or driving—just attach your leash or seat belt. Designed with the help of a veterinarian, it's great for all small dogs except dachshunds. Contact: Preferred Pet Professionals, P.O. Box 40, Glenelg, MD 21737, (301) 531-3237. The Doggie Bag can also be ordered from: DuSay's, 215 Seventh Street, Picayune, MS 39466, (601) 798-9308. Remember: discretion is the better part of valor.

I'LL MEET YOU IN THE LOBBY

Three cheers and some tail-wagging for the American Dog Owners Association! The ADOA, established in 1970, works to better the lives of dogs and to protect the rights of their humans. The organization provides information to people about breeding, dog overpopulation, training, and the exhibiting of purebreds. In addition, it supports anti-dog theft programs, tries to stop puppy giveaway promotions, and lobbies and litigates to prevent dog fighting, negligent transportation of dogs, false advertising by dog food companies, and inhumane practices in the breeding of puppies for pet shops. To join the fight, contact: American Dog Owners Association, Inc., 1920 Route 9, Castleton, NY 12053, (518) 477-8469.

MEASURING UP

Feeling tall is easier when you can rely on the accuracy of your progress reports. Farm & Country Marketing makes a measuring stick that's every inch a winner. Accurate, divided into ¼″ increments, and measuring dogs up to 36″ tall, it disassembles for easy storage. Farm & Country also makes an easy-to-install and easy-to-remove self-anchoring stake with the tenacity of a bulldog for maximum safety. To find out more, write: Farm & Country Marketing, P.O. Box 277, Fort Atkinson, WI 53538, (414) 563-3836.

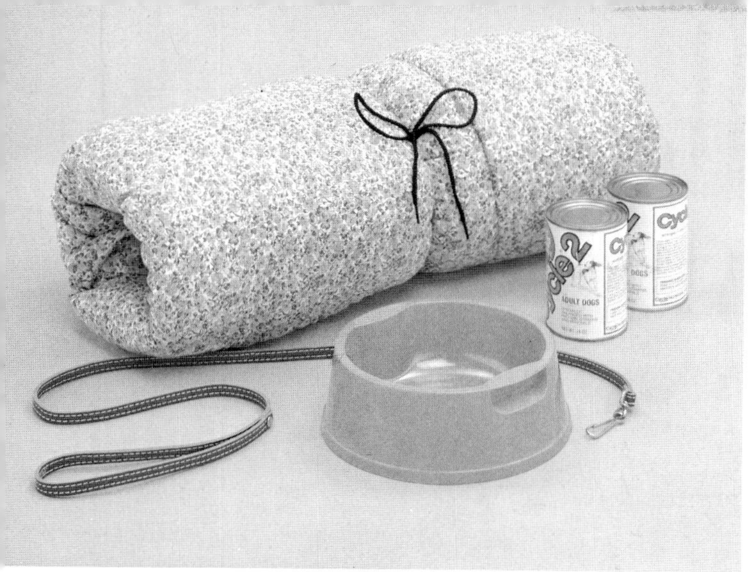

The Pet-Sac, rolled and ready to go.

Fritz and the Doggie Bag Sleepsac.

BAGGING A BARGAIN

Becky Bearry's husband wouldn't let Fritz sleep in their bed, so Becky and Fritz, an inventive dachshund, designed the perfect answer—a sleeping bag. The result, the *Doggie Bag Sleepsac*, is sold by Penny Quinn Products, and a similar item, the *Pet-Sac*, is sold by Pet-Agree. Both are perfect for the dog with very territorial people or for the dog who just wants a place of his own. Comfortable for daytime use as well as for sleeping, they can be used in cars or on carpets and are machine washable. The Pet-Sac has a printed fabric outer shell and a brushed nylon tricot lining. It comes in two sizes: regular, which measures 30″ × 16″ and unzips to measure 30″ × 32″; and large, which is 30″ × 24″ zipped and 30″ × 48″ unzipped.

Penny Quinn's Doggie Bag Sleepsac comes in blue cotton denim and off-white natural canvas. The four sizes begin at $23.95, and your name can be stenciled on the outside for an additional $4. For information on the Pet-Sac, contact: Pet-Agree Co., P.O. Box 926, East Brunswick, NJ 08816, (201) 254-8064. For information on the Doggie Bag Sleepsac, contact: Penny Quinn Products, P.O. Box 5381, Auburn, CA 95604, (916) 823-7690.

Puttin' On The Spitz

Still undiscovered by film makers, Shetland Sheepdog Lazer is a sensation in the Big Apple. Winner of the 1984 "Most Wonderful Pet" contest at Radio City Music Hall, he beat thirty-one other pets to become the spokesdog for the Pets Are Wonderful (PAW) Council. Lazer, known as "The Wonderdog" to his adoring fans and his manager, Tom Roczen, has appeared as a guest on a number of local and national television shows and was Carnation's Mr. May for the 1984 Mighty Dog calendar. This charismatic nine-year-old dresses to impress, doning top hat and tails for performances or nights on the town. He can do over forty tricks, including answering the telephone and replacing the receiver when Roczen has finished speaking, turning on the TV, finding his dish, sneezing on command, counting to five, opening a book, peeling a banana, walking backwards, shaking with his right or left paw, and bowing with his cane in his mouth. Not only can he perform all these stunts to verbal commands, but he responds to hand signals as well. Not bad, Lazer.

For information on Lazer's personal appearances, contact manager Tom Roczen at: 105-16 Flatlands First St., Brooklyn, NY 11236, (718) 763-0967.

Off the Collar

EVEN GUARD DOGS CAN USE A DOGGUARD

It's a lot of fun to put your head out the window when you're driving, and sometimes you're tempted to leap right out of the window to chase something or to follow your people, but you shouldn't ever do these things. They can be extremely dangerous, and sometimes will power isn't enough to help you resist temptation. Ray Allen's three types of DogGuard window guards will keep you safely inside the car even when your mischievous impulses get the better of you. They fit almost any types of window and install and dismantle in seconds. To order, contact: Ray Allen Manufacturing Co., Inc., P.O. Box 9281, 310 Tia Juana, Colorado Springs, CO 80932, (303) 633-0404.

Lost and Found

The best way to find yourself, of course, is never getting lost in the first place. However, ten million dogs and cats get lost every year, and sixty-five to ninety percent of them never reach home again. Some are killed in accidents; others are euthanized in overcrowded shelters. Some starve; others find new people to love, but they spend the rest of their lives wondering what happened to their old ones. All dogs, especially puppies, with their limitless curiosity and limited sense of direction, should adhere to a few simple rules...

►When you take a walk, always use a leash. The collar should be snug, but comfortable enought to allow a person to place two fingers between the collar and your neck.

►When exercising alone, stay in a yard, preferably one with a fence that's high and has no room for squeezing or digging through or under.

►If there is no fence, limit yourself in some other way. Staying tethered to a stake driven 18-24" into the ground is one way to keep your mind from wandering and your body from following. A lightweight chain attached to a cable strung between two trees is another.

If, however, you get lost despite these precautions, a little foresight could come in very handy. If you haven't done so already, you should make use of a registry as soon as possible, so that if you do lose your way or are dognapped, you have a good chance of making it home.

Both the Purina Puppy Chow Lost Pet Program and Animal Trackers, Inc. provide I.D. tags for concientious dogs. If someone finds you, the toll-free, 24-hour phone number can be called. The number on your tag identifies you and your person, and the operator will try to reach your home. If no one answers, friends, colleagues, and even your veterinarian will be called in an attempt to find your owner. If at first no one who can take you home can be reached, the Purina program will make arrangements, either with your finder or with a local animal shelter or veterinarian, for your temporary housing and, if necessary, medical care. The Purina Puppy Chow Lost Pet Program is headed by Brian Lynch, who was inspired by the loss of his cockapoo, Miss Jenny, to found a national hotline for lost dogs. (Miss Jenny returned home safely.) Initial registration is $6.95, and yearly renewal costs $2.95. Fifty-five cents of each registration fee is donated to local humane societies. For more information, call 1-800-FIND-PET. Registration with Animal Trackers costs $10 for one year and $20 for five years. Contact: Animal Trackers, P.O. Box 8427, Santa Cruz, Ca 95061, (408) 438-5601.

Brian Lynch and Miss Jenny.

If you're afraid of losing an I.D. tag, you can opt instead for a permanent means of identification. Julie Moscove's Tatoo-A-Pet will place a number on your stomach or inside one of your legs in only a few minutes. The procedure is virtually painless, Tatoo-A-Pet operates nationwide, and ninety-nine percent of lost dogs with this company's tattoos have made it back home. Since the number each dog receives is not a human's social security number, but a code indicating the tattooist, the dog's state of residence, and the dog's individual registration number, your identity can be traced even if part of the tattoo is obliterated or changed by a dognapper. In addition, litters of puppies, who are most susceptible to such criminals, can be registered without having to be retattooed when they leave home to live with new people; the system centers on dogs rather than on humans. Registration costs $20; you will receive your own tattooed registration number, a tag with a 24-hour collect number, and decals for your home and your human's car to discourage dognappers. Tatoo-A-Pet offers free registration to dogs adopting senior citizens on fixed incomes and to dogs in animal shelters. In the latter case, the tattoo allows the humans running the shelters to make sure that dogs aren't taken to laboratories to be used in experiments or abandoned once they have left a shelter with a person. Police dogs, search-and-rescue dogs, and guide, service, and signal dogs also receive free registration. A complete description of every registered dog is kept on file, and Tatoo-A-Pet will attempt to trace any tattoo on a found animal, even if it is not the company's own marking. To register, write Tatoo-A-Pet, 1625 Emmons Ave., Brooklyn, NY 11235, or call: (718) 646-8200. If your humans wish to report finding a dog or cat with a tattoo, they should call (718) 646-8203 collect from New York or call (800) TATTOOS toll-free from any other state.

SELF-PRESERVATION

A good, brisk dog-paddle can be a lot of fun, and if you're around a boat, a pool, a beach, or a lake, it can save your life. But although most of us can swim, we also tire easily and have trouble staying afloat very long. That's why a life preserver, like Pet-Agree's **Pet Preserver**, can be so important. This one is light, comfortable, adjustable, and perfect for the athletic dog who's not afraid to play it safe. To find out which of the four sizes is right for you, write or call: Pet-Agree Co., P.O. Box 926, East Brunswick, NJ 08816, (201) 254-8064.

Beat the Heat

Perhaps they were out in the sun a little too long, but they had an idea that was so crazy, it was wonderful—a canteen for dogs! The makers of the Pet Canteen realized that the Great Outdoors loses most of its appeal when you're panting and thirsty. It's not that your people don't try—they usually set out a shallow bowl of water—but it's just not enough. *The Pet Canteen* holds five quarts to let you drink as much as you like, and a special detachable dish holds 32 ounces of your favorite food as well. It won't tip, and it's lightweight and portable, so you can use it indoors, too. It's the perfect gift for hot dogs of all breeds. To order, send $14.95 for a canteen with a food dish or $12.95 for one without to: Pet Canteen, Inc., P.O. Box 335, Canoga Park, CA 91305. California residents must add sales tax.

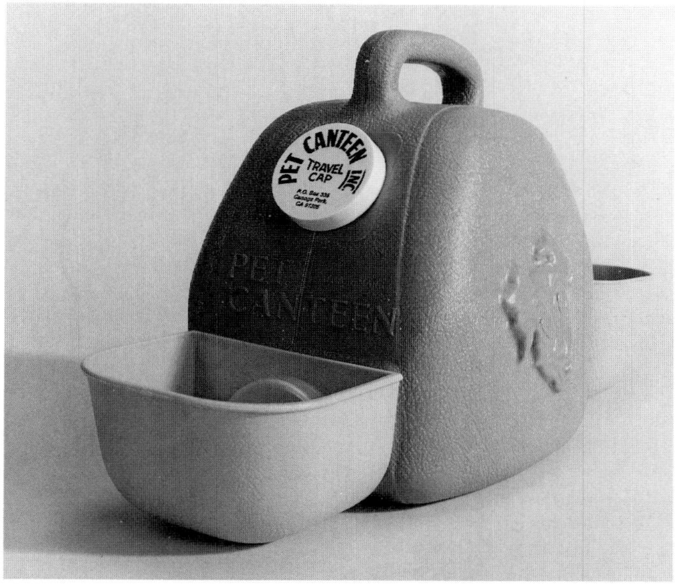
PET CANTEEN INC
TRAVEL CAP

LASSIE COME HOME

It's easy to lose track of time, especially when you're having fun. Sun Hill's *Watch Dog* tells you when it's time to go home by using a quartz LCD alarm. It sounds at a preset time for sixty seconds and can be reset or turned off easily. Just clip it onto your collar; it's water resistant and includes instructions on training yourself to respond to it. The average dog needs only ten days to master the technique. Who knows? Maybe the other dogs will think it's an emergency beeper. To order by mail, contact: Sun Hill Industries, Inc., Glendale Commerce Park, 48 Union Street, Stamford, CT 06906, (203) 324-7550. Retailers should contact: Shippan Distributors Inc. 176 Ocean Drive West, Stamford, CT 06902, (203) 356-1066. Watch Dog is not recommended for dogs who must navigate traffic.

Off the Collar

PET ROCKS, PART II

VIDEO DOG
VIDEO DOG
MEDICAL RECORD SHEET
VIDEO DOG WORLDS EASIEST PET!

At last, people allergic to dogs, tenants whose leases forbid pets, and those who don't have time to care for a dog can bask in the warmth of canine charm. Creative Programming's twenty-minute **Video Dog** does tricks, exercises itself, never needs to go outside in bad weather, and comes with an owner's manual, a medical record sheet, and a license. To order, write: Creative Programming, Inc., 30 East 60th Street, New York, New York, 10022 or call: (212) 688-9100.

The Saf-T-Truck Harness.

Fasten Seat Belts, Please

Submitted for your consideration: according to the Humane Society, more than 100,000 dogs are injured or killed each year because they ride in the backs of open pickup trucks without safety restraints. Those who don't fall from, jump from, or get thrown from these vehicles are often pelted with debris and insects, and even dogs riding inside cars travel in peril. All too often, the dogs themselves, through nervousness or recklessness, become the cause of accidents. Our recommendation: Custom Care Pet Supply's restraint systems. Small and medium-sized dogs can use the Saf-T-Car Seat. It comes in three sizes, includes a raised platform to give you full command of the road, and has a removable, covered water dish for your driving convenience. Its strength and safety will help you to relax and enjoy the ride, and it installs in seconds, so using it won't interrupt your busy schedule. For dogs over twenty-five pounds, Custom Care makes both a **Saf-T-Car Harness** and a **Saf-T-Truck Harness**. Each comes in five sizes. For more information, contact: Custom Care Pet Supply Inc., 8124 Holy Cross Place, Los Angeles, CA 90045, (213) 670-5344. A similar product is available from **Hamilton Halter**. It's a durable nylon strap that attaches to both the car seat belt and your own harness for maximum comfort and safety. At pet shops, or write: Hamilton Halter Mfg. Co., Inc., P.O. Box 6319, Ocala, FL 32678-6319; call: (904) 237-6188. Buckle up!

Sit'n Stay

Hamilton Halter's seat belt.

PICNIC PARAPHERNALIA

Nothing's more refreshing than eating outdoors, but when ants and other crawling insects get into our dishes, we wouldn't feed the results to a cat. There's no need to let bugs spoil your meal, though. An ingenious dish called the Superbowl uses a miniature moat to drown ants before they ever reach your food. The 14″ model, for larger dogs, costs $15 and comes in a rustic beige. A 10″ version for smaller dogs is $12; choose bright gold or red to reflect your brilliant personality. To order, contact Pal-O-Mine Products, Inc., "Superbowl" Dept. NP, P.O. Box 2152, Malibu, CA 90265, (203) 306-1194. California residents should add 6½% sales tax.

Bright Gear for Bright Dogs

Hunting is a great way to stay in shape, but it has its disadvantages—like dirt, cold, prickly bushes, and the chance that you'll be mistaken for the game. To prevent discomfort and danger, wear something bright and practical, like Paws 'n Shop's All-Weather Coat. It comes in fluorescent orange for hunting and nighttime use, as well as in tan, red, and navy. Velcro closures open and close easily and ensure a perfect fit; the water-repellant surface resists thorns and dirt as well as moisture, and the wool plaid lining takes the bite out of howling winds. Six sizes, priced from $29.95 to $43.95 and embroidered with your name in 12″-high letters, are available from: Paws 'n Shop, 23 Birchwood Circle, Bedford, N.H. 03102, (603) 622-0544.

A whole line of reflective accessories is made by Petsavers, a division of Jog-A-Lite. The coat, sold in eleven sizes to accommodate safety seekers of all types, is made of light yellow nylon twill with a highly reflective white strip around the front and sides. Waterproof and equipped with adjustable hook and loop straps, it can be purchased with either a fleece or a nylon lining. The reflective material used in all Petsavers products has 47,000 microprisms per square inch, resulting in a nighttime range of over 800 feet. It reflects wet or dry, is not faded by repeated washings, and reflects colored as well as white light.

Petsavers' collars have 360° reflectivity and are available with either a buckle or a hook and loop closure. Their strong tubular nylon webbing backs are designed to withstand the punishment an active dog's life can inflict. Eight sizes are designed to make sure there's a collar that fits you in comfort. Be sure to take a look at Petsavers' packs and 2′, 4′, and 6′ leashes as well; they'll be easy to pick out of the crowd. Write: Petsavers, A Division of Jog-A-Lite International, Inc., Box 125, Silver Lake, NH 03875. In New Hampshire, call: (603) 367-8273; elsewhere, call toll-free: (800) 258-8974.

CASEY

Casey models Paws 'n Shop's All-Weather Coat.

BEAM US UP, SCOTTY: HIGH-TECH HELP ARRIVES

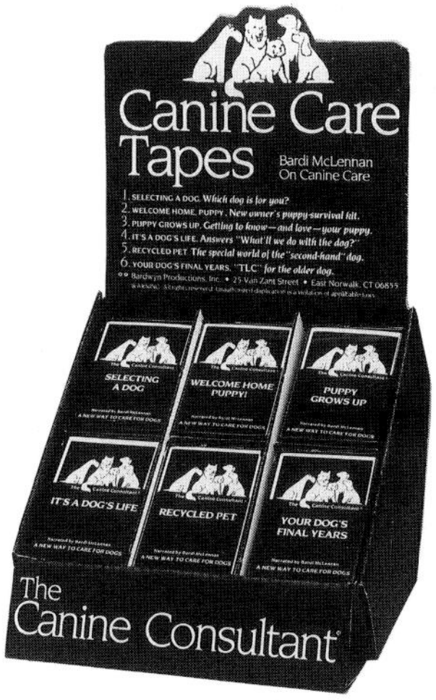
Canine Care
Tapes
Bardi McLennan
On Canine Care
The
Canine Consultant

It starts with little things, with behavior that's adorable at first, and you thoughtlessly encourage it. Or maybe you've simply ended up with the wrong person for your temperament and lifestyle. But, one way or another, you find that you're living with a human who has serious behavioral problems. Don't panic, though, and don't despair. You can avoid trouble in the future and break existing bad habits by making use of audio and video products to educate your humans.

The Canine Consultant, Bardi McLennan, offers six audio cassettes designed to correct the ignorance of well-meaning humans. Dogs, too, can profit from McLennan's valuable self-help information. The tapes cover everything from matching your temperament and your person's to curing carsickness, from surviving puppyhood with your person's affections intact to vacations and moving, and from adopting a second set of people to making the most of your declining years. Your humans should find the tapes informative, enjoyable, and easy to understand. To order, write: Bardwyn Productions, Inc., P.O. Box 5044, Westport, CT 06881-5044 or call: (203) 454-4300.

Dr. Dennis C. Fetko has also produced six audio cassettes for use in training humans. Fetko, also known as *Dr. Dog*, concentrates on educating people to understand a dog's needs and psychology. With a little luck and some help from Dr. Dog, your people may soon be bragging that you're not just *obedient*—you're well-behaved, even when they're not around. Fetko's tapes, which include such subjects as housebreaking, chewing, jumping, pulling, barking, and aggression, cost $12.95 each and can be ordered by writing: Dr. Fetko, Box 28176, San Diego, CA 92128 or by calling: (619) 485-7433.

***Puppy's First Year*, a videotape starring behaviorist Ann Childers, offers advice on health as well as behavior, including information on diet, grooming, dental care, dominant behavior, hip dysplasia, and leash training. Each copy costs $29.95 and may be ordered from: Media West Home Video, 10255 S.W. Arctic Drive, Beaverton OR 97005, (503) 626-7002.**

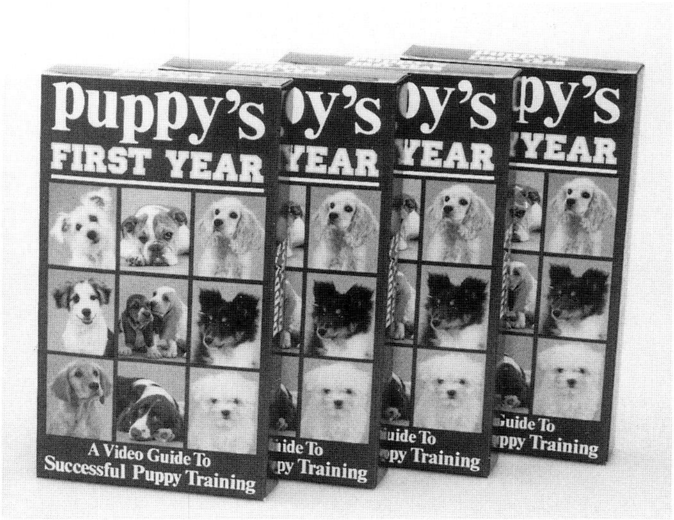
puppy's
FIRST YEAR
A Video Guide To
Successful Puppy Training

DINING IN

What's New for Gourmutts

by Betty Cocker

© RAEANNE RUBENSTEIN, 1987 TELEPHOTO

Have you noticed how crowded your supermarket aisles have become lately? The selection of choice tidbits, from biscuits and bones to kibble and canned food, from appetizers to scrumptious desserts and between-meal snacks, is getting wider and wider. No wonder, since pleasing your palate has become a multibillion-dollar industry and there are countless companies, large and small, vying to captivate your taste buds. It's enough to make you head for the nearest fast food outlet in total confusion, drooling all the way.

How to choose? Bearing in mind that you should be planning balanced, nutritious, and lip-smacking meals for any time of day or night, we've pawed through the latest offerings of a number of firms, taste-testing all of them to bring you suggestions for the best of the best. All you have to do is select what appeals and chow down. Some of the foods we've included may not be available at your local grocery store yet—you may have to hit the pet shop or gourmet center. But the extra trip will be well worth it. We've been especially careful to select *natural* products for you: products that contain no artificial flavors or fillers, and no artificial colors.

Superior Snacking

When you've got the munchies (and we all do from time to time), don't plead for people food. Most of the time it won't be good for you, and it'll spoil your digestion. Make sure, instead, to have good snacks on hand, snacks such as Delores Davie's crunchy **Growlnola Bars**. You won't find any chemicals or preservatives here; what you *will* find are satisfying, yummy treats in four sizes (according to your size) that will stop that gnawing feeling without upsetting your tender system. Growlnola Bars are available at supermarkets throughout western North America; if you have trouble finding them, write Growlnola, Inc., P.O. Box 70, Freeland, WA 98249, or call (206) 321-1708.

On the other side of the continent are Vermont's Carol and Jim Coski, breeders of quality Cocker Spaniels (a breed dear to my heart). They take special pains to insure that each pup grows up loving people as much as it does its litter mates. One of the side effects of this dog-human socializing is that each puppy also grows up with a razor-sharp nose for the good life: these spaniels really know what they like. And what they like is natural food, without unpronounceable additives or harmful salt and sugar. To cater to these canny canines, Jim and Carol have developed a variety of dog cookies guaranteed to please even the most jaded taste buds. **Coski's Cookies** come in ten flavors, including Liver Hydrants, Veggie Acorns, Chocolate Babies, and Apple Cinnamon Hearts. All are baked in the Coskis' own kitchen, though they're becoming so popular that expansion is inevitable. You can buy the yummies from Petworthies Ltd., 4 Brookside Place, Westport, CT 06880; (203) 227-0187, or write Coski's Canine Cookies, P.O. Box 544, Bellows Falls, VT 05101.

Variety is the spice of life, and what better place to put the spice than in a selection of hors d'oeuvres to serve to guests or bring along as

ALL NATURAL
DOG COOKIES
NO PRESERVATIVES ADDED
COSKI'S CHOICE
Famous
PET TREATS

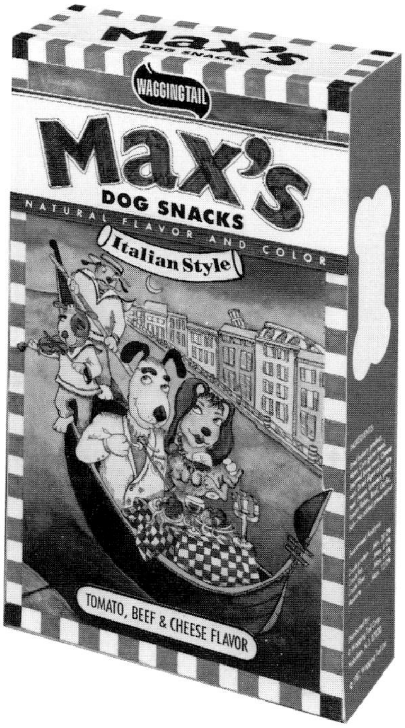
WAGGINGTAIL
Max's
DOG SNACKS
NATURAL FLAVOR AND COLOR
Italian Style
TOMATO, BEEF & CHEESE FLAVOR

a hostess gift when you're invited out? **Max's Dog Snacks** fill the bill. They come in Italian (tomato, beef, and cheese), American (beef, cheese, and bacon), Yuppie (mesquite-grilled chicken), and Christmas (turkey, of course) flavors. Custom spices like basil and garlic are added to the wholesome flour, corn, and bonemeal base. Available at finer pet and gourmet shops, gift shops, and natural food stores, or contact: Wagging Tail Ltd., 206 Garden Street, Hoboken, NJ 07030; phone (201) 656-0202.

If the tang of the salt air and the feel of the sea breeze on your fur are particular pleasures, try something new for snacking that comes from the ocean deeps. (Yes, we do mean fish. Our kitty nemeses have known how good it is for years, but have managed to make us turn up our noses at it.) Dust off your spirit of adventure, ignore the catcalling, and taste a **Norwegian Sea Snack**. Made of 100% cod netted in frigid arctic waters, Norwegian Sea Snacks are particularly high in protein and low in fat. But best of all, they taste delicious (really!). You'll find Norwegian Sea Snacks at better pet shops, or call Scandinavian American Marketing, Inc., at (415) 921-3500 for an outlet near you. (The address, should you wish to drop a card, is 2228 Union Street, San Francisco, CA 94123.)

You may have been trying to keep it a secret, but we know that mint is one of your favorite flavors. Trouble is, up to now you've had to cadge peppermint candies from your owners when they were in a beneficent mood. And the trouble with *that* is that people candy really isn't good for you. (The sugar can rot your teeth before their time.) But finally somebody understands your craving. **Granpaws Mutt Mints** are all-natural and have a delicate mint flavor and aroma that's irresistible. Best of all, they contain only 16 calories each.. Granpaw also makes a richer **Doggie Cookie** by eliminating the mint and adding milk and eggs for more protein. Both are baked by Clever Endeavors Bakery Co., P.O. Box 6058, Anaheim, CA 92806. They are shown with **Bowser Chicken Biscuits**, made of whole chickens, wheat, corn, and seasonings from an old family recipe. The bakers are Bowser Biscuits Inc., Rt. 1, Box 259, Plymouth, WI 53073.

HEALTH TREATS
NORWEGIAN
Sea Snacks
FOR DOGS
100% Fish
No Additives
67% Protein
Pure and Healthy
Love at First Bite

BRADLEY OLMAN

Dishing It Up

Even when you've chosen the tastiest, healthiest snacks and entrees, they can lose some of their appeal without the proper table setting. **Curzon Designs** makes matching dishes and place mats that will have your guests applauding your

DINING IN

GRANPAWS
MUTT MINTS
With All Natural Ingredients
Bone Appetit
BOWSER
CHICKEN
BISCUITS
Bone Appetit
GRANPAWS
DOGGIE COOKIES
All Natural Doggie Treats

BRADLEY OLMAN

good taste. "Bone Appetit" features a cheerful blue-and-white design on a porcelain bowl and wipe-clean mat. Other designs offered include "Good Dog" and "Woof." (There are even motifs for cats.) Bowls come in 7″ and 9″ diameters; mats, a roomy 17½″ by 11¾″, so spills won't be a problem. From Curzon Designs Ltd., 561 R Acorn St., Box ZZ, Deer Park, NY 11729; (800) 222-4188, or (516) 242-1202.

Devotees of classic styling will love the sophisticated marbleized dishes from **Imperial Pet Products**. Made of a heavy-duty substance called "acrilean marble," the dishes are wear and spill resistant and come in four fashionable color combinations—brown/white, blue/white, black/gray, and white/gray—to harmonize with any decor. Choose the size that's right for you:

one-cup, two-cup, four-cup, or eight-cup. On display at pet shops, grooming shops, and kennels, or order from Imperial Pet Products, P.O. Box 157, Walnutport, PA 18088. Phone (215) 435-6130.

If you're a medium-sized canine, you may have looked with longing at pals who are substantially bigger than you, envying their ability to peek at what's laid out on the kitchen counter or dining room table for dinner. But as any Dane, Newfie, or Mastiff can tell you, being big isn't all it's cracked up to be. Some veterinarians suggest that height poses special digestive problems for large dogs, causing undue strain when they eat dinner off the floor. **Paws 'n Shop** raises the issue with double-diner crocks that fit snugly into a chrome-plated tray. The tray boosts the bowls several inches closer to your nose, thus reducing strain, and has a convenient handle and no-skid rubber feet. The crocks come in ivory or rust, in 13- or 48-ounce sizes, and are made of unbreakable polypropylene that's dishwasher safe. Order from Paws 'n Shop, 23 Birchwood Circle, Bedford, NH 03102; (603) 622-0544.

And for the Main Course . . . .

Choosing the right table setting is one thing; selecting the right entree is something else entirely. What you eat as your main meal of the day will depend on your age, breed, size, and occupation. If you read the labels on many conventional foods, both canned and dry, you'll find mysterious ingredients that may do your sensitive digestive tract no good at all. And if you're like me, you'll steer clear of soy derivatives (I'm allergic to them, as are many of my friends). But happily there are many other choices on those crowded supermarket aisles. Following are what we consider to be among the best *natural* entrees available, the products of years of research and testing.

Puppies have special nutritional needs; their food must be easily digestible, yet chock-full of vitamins and protein for strong bones, good teeth, and healthy coats. **ANF Puppy Food** meets all requirements: it's crammed with chicken and egg protein and provides all essential vitamins and minerals, obviating the need for supplements. This superb kibble is sold in pet and feed stores, veterinary clinics, and breeding and boarding kennels. If you have trou-